Basic Facts

FOR CREATING EFFECTIVE
ART/DESIGN ▪ ADVERTISING ▪ PRINTING

~

WILLIAM J. STEVENS

~

THE DORVAL COMPANY, INC.

BASIC FACTS FOR CREATING EFFECTIVE ART/DESIGN, ADVERTISING, PRINTING.
Copyright 1996, by William J. Stevens. Printed and bound in the United
States of America. All rights reserved. No part of this book may be
reproduced in any form or by any electronic or mechanical means including
photocopy, information storage or retrieval systems without permission in
writing from the publisher, except by a reviewer who may quote brief
passages in a review. Published by The Dorval Company Inc., 4575 Barclay
Crescent, Lake Worth, FL 33463. First edition. Paperback printing 1996.

Stevens, William J.
BASIC FACTS for Creating Effective Art/Design, Advertising, Printing.
Includes Glossary
ISBN 1-888154-50-0
1. Authorship. I. Title   Library of Congress No. 95-71662

Dedicated to

DORothy VALentine Stevens

DORVAL

The first three letters of her name

ensure that she is on my mind

constantly.

A COMPENDIUM OF IDEAS
AND PRACTICES FOR ALL
PRACTITIONERS OF THE
PRINTED WORD

If... the basic fundamentals of art and copy produced by artists, designers, and advertising agencies were thoroughly understood and then diligently applied, most of the printed reproduction and readability headaches would be cured.

James P. DeLuca

Dr. James P. DeLuca,
Chairman, Department of Graphic Arts
and Advertising Technology
New York City Technical College

Acknowledgments

This book, in many ways, is truly a labor of love. First, it reflects my love and respect for the graphic arts industry. I started by sweeping the floor in the linotype plant of Ruttle, Shaw & Wetherill, Philadelphia, PA. From that humble beginning and with the help of Fritz Peters, foreman, it was straight up the ladder. Some of my "helpers" along the way were, Jerome Marcus, Henry Chenny, Ray Blattenberger, Walter E. Soderstrom, Jim McClay, Milton Hudders, Lee Augustine, Tom Morgan, C. M. Baker, Harold Geggenheimer, Jim McClintick, Carl Mellick, Bert Bassett, George Houck, Edwin McAmis, Dorothy Meyerman, "O. Mike" Fichera, NAPL, NPES, ASAE, and a hundred other individuals and the trade press, who have helped to shape my working life.

Then there are my "very special friends." I will not be the first nor the last to say that without friends, you have nothing. When my wife Dorothy passed into heaven after 42 years of a beautiful marriage, I needed friends. Bishop John (Mort) Smith, now of Pensacola, FL, gave me the support that comes only once in a lifetime. And he does it to this day. The kind, strong hands of Rev. Francis Heinen, the love of Rev. Lewis Papara, Rev. Thomas Iwanowski, and the entire family of St. Joseph's Church in Oradell, NJ are still holding my hands.

Then there are my personal friends: The entire Machorek family, especially Margaret, Gloria and Al DeStefano, Stanley and Alice Miller, the George Arnold family, the Offner's, the Feldeisen family (all 14), the Thompson's, Sidney and Helen Druce, the Giovanisci's, Lois and Bill Haug, Marijane and Fred Singer, Sister Joan Schmidt, Jim and Terry DeLuca. Is this my "Christmas List?" No, not really. These and many more beautiful friends have kept, and still are helping me, keep my faith in humanity.

Thank you all for keeping my life a real joy. Thanks too, to my editor, Grace Michael and to my consultants, Ed and Jane Owen and Betty Wright. I could not have published this book without your help.

INTRODUCTION

In the beginning, there was the printer, with hand-set type, and sheets hand-fed on a foot treadle power printing press. Glamorous, revolutionary so people thought in those days.

Four color printing by letterpress? What is that? You must be dreaming! It will never happen.

Offset printing? Another dream? Not so for Harris, Seybold, Potter, Webendorfer, Miehle and a few other visionaries of the past.

Over the years, these dreams became a reality. But wait, the best and probably the impossible is yet to come. The artist with multi-colors at his disposal, and camera ready copy for the printer, is no longer a dream. The advertising agency who could offer four-color printing, is no longer a dream either. Then came the high-powered salesmen who would promise that their plant could produce printing in any color on any material, even on cloth and plastic! These too were no longer dreams.

As Mr. Barnum would say, "You ain't seen nothin' yet!" The age of the computer, recycled paper, 600+ line screened photographs, digital and waterless dry offset printing, stochastic screening. When will this printing phenomenon stop? Probably never. If Gutenberg were alive today he would probably say, "Why didn't I think of that?" It's quite likely that the future may well be — ALL IN THE MIND.

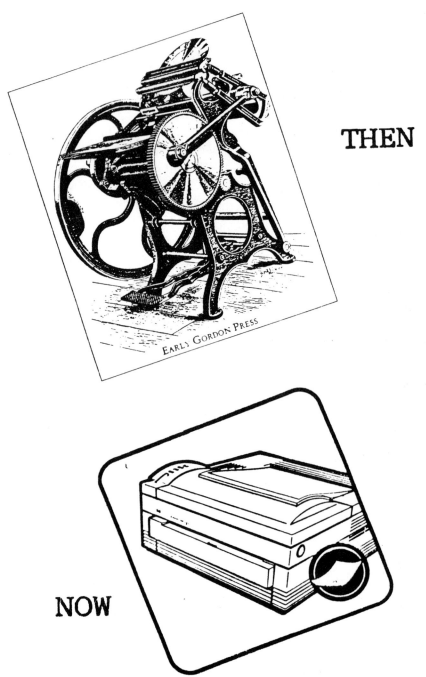

"Copyright (Year of copyright) Hewlett-Packard Company
Reproduced with Permission"

Basic Facts

Table of Contents

Chapter		Page
1	PRINTING SELLS PRODUCTS & SERVICES	1
2	DESIGNING FOR PRINT	7
3	METALLIC OR SHEEN INK	11
4	PLANNING PHOTOGRAPHY FOR PRINTING	15
5	WAYS TO PROTECT PHOTOGRAPHS	17
6	PERIODS AND HYPHENS	21
7	OUT OF REGISTER, WHITE LETTERS	25
8	BORDERS, RULES AND DOTS	29
9	PRODUCING ANNUAL REPORTS	33
10	BINDING PERFECT BOUND BOOKS	40
11	TRADE SHOW ADVERTISING	45
12	UPGRADING NEWSPAPER ADS	49
13	DIRECT DIGITAL COLOR SEPARATIONS	55
14	STOCHASTIC SCREENING	59
15	"LIVE" DEMONSTRATIONS	63
16	TRADE MARK ASSOCIATION	67
17	PRINTING TRADE PRACTICES, REVISED	73
18	NEW TELEMARKETING SALES RULES	79
19	GENERAL GLOSSARY	83
20	PARTIAL LIST PREPRESS TERMS	93

Basic Facts

Chapter 1

PRINTING SELLS PRODUCTS AND SERVICES

Recession, depression, inflation or whatever you wish to call it, it's still a most serious problem that hits hard at the economy of all Americans. It's no longer the problem of saving a little for a rainy day, the issue is one of having sufficient funds to exist from day to day. Ask any unemployed worker.

How many industries can possibly weather the storm? Layoffs mean more people in welfare lines. The word "worry" has now been supplanted by the word "FEAR!"

Our daily lives bring many kinds of fear: our shrinking bank accounts, the quality of our food, the "threatening" media, ever-rising medical bills. And there is the on-going fear that government will tax us right into the poorhouse. Concrete examples of each of these fears are clearly evident in the nation's daily newspapers.

The media too, at every level and in every form, are frightened. From the top brass to the computer operator, many are frightened about losing their jobs. WHY? Because the manufacturers of products and services are not selling the quantities produced. Put it another way, the public's not buying at the same rate as a few years ago. A surge of buying at certain holiday periods is not an indication of a stable economy.

PRINTING SELLS PRODUCTS & SERVICES

When senior executives in advertising agencies are worried, then the whole empire begins to shake, including the staff AND their clients. Thousands of agency accounts are cutting back on spending; this goes for the entire run of media: newspapers, radio, magazines, and even television. The news is not good.

Even top economists are doing some rethinking, including those in the printing industry. They stated first that a significant recovery would come in the first quarter of 1992, then they revised their thinking and predicted that perhaps a recovery would come about in the last quarter of 1992. And now, the hedge is toward the end of 1993, but the word "significant" has been eliminated by nearly every forecaster. Budgets, are budgets, are budgets, the one thing we know for sure is that they will be cut!

Advertising in magazines is down nearly 6 percent on the average. Some magazines have gone into Chapter 11, or worse, completely out of business.

If magazines don't sell copies, it hurts the printing industry.

If auto manufacturers don't sell cars, it hurts the printing industry.

If Campbell's doesn't sell soup, it hurts the printing industry.

If Hathaway's doesn't sell shirts, it hurts the printing industry.

AND IF PRINTERS STAND STILL, IT HURTS THE PRINTING INDUSTRY.

Many consumers are not buying the products they can't really afford, but they are sitting on the sidelines waiting to see what happens. The question is, how long can they wait?

All of these facts paint a rather negative picture, and it IS. Yet, for the printing industry, while there IS a better way, it won't happen unless the industry MAKES IT HAPPEN.

PRINTING SELLS PRODUCTS & SERVICES

For hundreds of years, ONE industry, ONE group, or ONE genius has weathered the storm; each met competition head on. THE GRAPHIC ARTS INDUSTRY CAN DO NO LESS!

During the past three years, dozens of printing plants have merged. Is this the way to "buy" accounts? It may be. The surviving firm surely must do a super job of advertising or it, too, will fall by the wayside, and many have. The printing industry has proven itself as a competitive industry and a turnaround is more than just possible.

David Ogilvy, advertising's greatest living legend, states it this way: "In this pervasive area of fear, who can create great advertising? The only good thing that can emerge from this period of terror is that it may result in a move away from silly advertising and start a trend towards the kind of advertising that SELLS. Housewives don't buy a detergent because the manufacturers' spokesperson told a joke on television last night. THEY BUY BECAUSE "IT PROMISES A BENEFIT."

PRINTING PROMISES A REAL BENEFIT. IT SELLS PRODUCTS AND SERVICES, and this fact can't be denied!

Manufacturing is currently experiencing fierce competition from overseas. Yet, we see some turnaround in this monumental problem.

Many companies are bringing major manufacturing back to America from Asia, Japan and Korea. Considering tariffs, freight, waiting time to have goods manufactured, and quality, it does appear that the benefit of "MADE IN AMERICA" is beginning to make sense.

Printing, as well, brings a major benefit. Printing can produce an end product like no other. From a can label to a newspaper and from a cereal carton to a theatre ticket, printing is with us every step of the way. Where would the average American be without a telephone directory, a product instruction manual or a daily newspaper?

PRINTING SELLS PRODUCTS & SERVICES

Telling printers that they should advertise is fine, but the problem goes much deeper. They must advertise the ENTIRE INDUSTRY, not simply their own company.

Advertise where? Why not in THE NEW YORK TIMES, THE WALL STREET JOURNAL, LOCAL NEWSPAPERS or even TELEVISION? PRINTING SELLS PRODUCTS AND SERVICES!

The graphic arts industry is capable of producing any quantity of printing needed by any consumer. This being a fact, why then are so many of our plants suffering from a lack of business? The answer is UNDER-DEMAND. This is the greatest challenge to all of us and we must find the way to increase the use of our product. And ADVERTISING IN ALL MEDIA is our best salesman.

It is our business to help the printing industry to remain stable and healthy. In the years ahead, more trained manpower will be needed in our nation's plants. But without a STRONG AND VIBRANT INDUSTRY, graduates of our schools and colleges, and workers who are sitting on a bench, waiting to be called, may discover that jobs are difficult to find.

The United States has ample reserve of scientific knowledge to create the machinery and electronic devices to master the equipment for production in all fields of our industry, and at super speed. This capability is obvious at every industry machinery exhibit.

Yes, current statistics prove that the printing business is basically healthy. However, from the point of view of profit versus the cost of doing business, some serious problems do arise. Granted, most costs in many industries are going up and few, if any, have come down. How then can this situation be reversed?

One newspaper, "USA TODAY," is biting the bullet. They are

PRINTING SELLS PRODUCTS & SERVICES

now suggesting to their advertisers that PRINT is the way to go! They will offer advertisers ads made directly from TV tape or other video sources. This will save advertisers thousands of dollars by not needing to go back to raw art for newspaper ads. A novel idea? Yes, but more so, "USA TODAY" is advertising PRINT.

The American public must help us to meet the challenge of UNDER-DEMAND. From third grade readers to high school and college texts to financial news letters, reading IS printing! And WE MUST SHOW, by every means of advertising available to us that printing is a vital part of our life-style and it does, indeed, educate and SELL PRODUCTS AND SERVICES.

PRINTING SELLS...
PRODUCTS AND SERVICES
WHEN ADVERTISING - USE PRINTING

Basic Facts — Chapter 2

DESIGNING FOR PRINT

Are the "good old days" of readable typography and design really gone? They laughed when I said that Cheltenham would come back as a good, readable type face, they're not laughing anymore. They are using Cheltenham!

It all comes down to "modern" design with "modern" typesetting attached to it in advertising. If the word "readability" were used in conjunction with modern design and typography, it might be a different ball game.

It makes little difference as to what service or product you are trying to sell, some type faces will be better suited for ads than others. No undertaker sells caskets! He sells a service, and his ad better not use Cooper Black. His ad type face must be dignified but above all it must be READABLE. Modern design and modern typesetting ARE IN, but let us NOT LEAVE OUT READABILITY.

I get dozens of ads on my desk every day, many of which find their way into the shredder as fast as you can say, "next." Here are some actual examples that might make good material for a late night stand-up comic.

A beautiful, four-color 8" x 10" ad was run in a prestigious

DESIGNING FOR PRINT

magazine. The ad extolled the virtues of a clear, almost white, light blue sky in the hills of the Smokies. The lodge that ran the ad was down in the valley and hardly noticeable. Noticeable? Neither were the words, "Come Visit Us," which were in WHITE REVERSE LETTERS IN AN ALMOST WHITE SKY. Was the design or the typography wrong? BOTH! It's really hard to understand why this "ERROR" wasn't caught by someone before it got to me. Since the ad was in four colors, a solid blue or even a black would have been easier to read.

The months of April and May are the mail carriers' test for back strain. Annual reports by the hundreds stream in on each trip. Designers have a field day with annual reports. From embossed to thermographed covers, to glassine fly sheets, to gold or silver stamping, they are all eye-catching. But then comes the inside, again a field day for designers.

I received an annual report from a Fortune 500 company (in which I have 2 shares of stock) and I thought I had lost my eyesight. Here is the scene:

On pages 4, 5 and 6 there were rows of three to a page, 2" x 2" photos of top management from vice president of management to vice president of waste disposal. How did I know their occupation? Their dress gave it away. The corporate title of each person was under the photo, PRINTED IN 6-POINT SILVER INK! Thank heaven for my magnifying glass which assured me that my eyesight was normal.

There were other solid colors in this report. A clean blue would have been readable and the 6-point type could have been increased to 8 point.

Here is a fourth scene: Another 8" X 10" ad. A beautiful clubhouse, luscious golf greens, a place that you want to call right away to make a reservation. Of course you would; they tell you so in the ad, in BIG 36-point Brush script style type. They say,

DESIGNING FOR PRINT

"DON'T WAIT, CALL US RIGHT NOW!" I would have too, but I would have to call information first. You see, THEY LEFT THE PHONE NUMBER OUT OF THE AD.

Experimentation with type faces may be justified, but one must consider READABILITY!

Oh, yes, I almost forgot my pet peeve. Six-point BODONI type in REVERSE run in four colors on a web press! Read it? Of course not, it looked like a single line of smudge. Change this? Of course. Instead of using six point, use eight or even ten point. And change the BODONI to a sans serif type, such as a GOTHIC or HELVETICA. Perhaps the best advice is this: for web presses, don't try four-color reverse type in very small sizes; you risk having a registration problem at high press speeds. And web presses run at amazingly high speeds, much faster than sheet fed presses.

Are changes needed? YES! TYPOGRAPHER and DESIGNER, let's make some changes. READABILITY SELLS products and services like NOTHING ELSE!

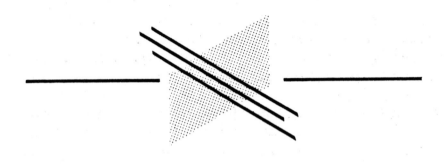

Basic Facts

Chapter 3

METALLIC OR SHEEN INK

SELLING IS SELLING — IS SELLING — IS SELLING, and sometimes, more often than not, just one bright idea can be the missing link to thousands and thousands of dollars in product or service sales. Catchy phrases, two word bombs, a fantastic studio shot, what comes next! PRINT IT! Hold on, not so fast — before you say print it, a lot more needs to be considered. READABILITY, for example. If the ad or brochure can't be read, easily, then the whole reason for advertising is lost. It's amazing how much advertising is so hard to read. A number of magazines beamed at the advertising industry stating their concern about hard to read advertising.

The artist says, "Boy, this will make a great ad" as he allows the address and the telephone number to be sent to the printer in six point, four color reverse type. A real problem in printing production. BUT THERE IS A BETTER WAY.

Another artist decides to run a twelve point italic serif type in capital letters in a very light pink solid. Of course you can't read it. Another problem. BUT THERE IS A BETTER WAY.

Then there is the customer who wants his sales message in white letters in a pale blue-white background cloud which hangs over his building now and then. He probably had sky

METALLIC OR SHEEN INK

writing in his mind, but it just will not work. And neither will small letter reverses in plain silver be readable. BUT THERE IS A BETTER WAY.

My research reveals that more advertisers are becoming aware of the problem of reverse letters in solids and backgrounds of multicolor ads. The problem is caused by misregister, slight as it may be.

Trying to obtain a PERFECT white letter in printing with four colors, one color over the other, can be a problem especially on very high speed web presses. The risk of distortion is high, especially in phone numbers and addresses which are traditionally set in small type. Why use small type? I'm told it just happens, not a real good reason at all.

So much for typography and design. What is this "BETTER WAY?" USE A TOOL OF THE TRADE THAT HAS BEEN AROUND FOR YEARS!

Many years ago, when as plant superintendent of a printing company, we had to print a multicolor self promotion piece, we were torn between running three colors or two colors. An ink salesman made a suggestion. Use a blue SHEEN METALLIC ink. We followed his suggestion to the letter. In essence we had a three color job by running only two colors. First, we had a nice silver-blue color for the solids, then this same blue gave us clean sharp reverses and finally we had black type over the blue which was easy to read.

Our artwork was prepared using the sheen ink theory. When printed we really had the appearance of a three color job. Our salesmen had a field day selling this "new found color system."

Take a look at the ads and promotional material of such firms as, Mazda, Hertz, Digital, Diners Club, Akiyama, Southern Bell, Franklin Printing Co., Mueller Martini, Chrysler and dozens more.

METALLIC OR SHEEN INK

They all have one more thing in common. Silver, gold, copper or other base colors of metallic inks. They stand out in any publication, door-to-door flyers, annual reports, greeting cards, direct mail or packaging. The PRODUCT USE is virtually endless and a good designer can work wonders.

Does it require some imagination on the part of the artist to use sheen inks? Yes, it does, but isn't imagination part of an artist's work? Sure it is. Actually he will be using a new found tool of the industry, or perhaps I should say a "REDISCOVERED" tool.

What is a SHEEN ink? Sheen means shininess, brightness, and luster. Sheen is any color that has these combined qualities. One ink company calls it "metal sheen" and another firm calls it "metallic ink matching system." They all have a full range of colors: rich gold, pale gold, blues, greens, reds, and purple too. All with ONE impression and all have a metallic base.

SHEEN ink is the basis of A BETTER WAY! It is possible to run small letters in reverse type because you are running only a single color. There is no problem with overprinting since sheen colors are lighter than full bodied colors. The actual density of the sheen ink can be modified to suit any particular job. It is also easy to develop various shades or tints for background or large reverse letters. Agencies are finding out that sheen colors have a new found eye appeal. You can do wonders with good typography and of course good design and good photographs. However, when you need that "extra touch" of EYE CONTACT for an ad or brochure or product, use a sheen ink. It will make your message pop out and SELL your product. It's a new twist to an old sales tool for printers, artists and advertisers and IT REALLY WORKS!

PRINTING SELLS...
PRODUCTS AND SERVICES
WHEN ADVERTISING - USE PRINTING

Basic Facts

Chapter 4

PLANNING PHOTOGRAPHY FOR PRINTING

"The more 'BASICS' change, the more 'BASICS' remain the same." In the reproduction process, no matter what method is used, nothing has ever changed from having a good "workable" photograph.

Even with today's ultra modern, sophisticated and digital methods, of creating a photographic image, the end result is not always perfect. Nor, in the broadest sense does it portray what was intended.

Fashion photography, for example, still needs massive retouching (airbrushing) to develop a usable print. In a most prestigious magazine, a model sitting on a bench near a bridge was completely obscured by the bridge. Was the client selling the bridge? No, he was selling a hair spray. It was a windy scene, yet the model's hair was under control. Airbrushing of the bridge came to the rescue for the next printing. Sad? But it's true!

It takes artistry with a camera to illustrate a fact, create an impression or tell a story photographically. It takes craftsmanship to make allowances for the changes that inevitably take place in each step from the original film, to a photographic print, to a computer, and finally to the dots of ink on a sheet of paper.

PLANNING PHOTOGRAPHY FOR PRINTING

The ideal photographs for reproduction are those planned from the beginning with one eye on the final reproduced form. In the normal rush of producing material for publication, there is often little opportunity to think about the reproduction qualities of a photograph until prints are seen. At the time the photograph is taken, by all means, plan for good reproduction before the shutter is opened. A little extra time spent on good photography can save hours of time for costly and sometimes unsatisfactory retouching.

It is no small wonder that studio photographers, when they are shooting a model or a chair, will take a series of shots with different lighting and positions. They are looking for perfection.

The making of a good photographic print will go a long way toward getting better reproduction, no matter what reproduction method is used.

Newspapers, for example, will take almost any print supplied. And, in general they like an "overall" screened background. Frankly, this does nothing for a chair! Look at a "Lord and Taylor" ad. You will see only a hint of background screen, if any. Yet the subject matter in the ad stands out from the rest of the page.

Glossy, white prints which get all of the details out of the negative are best for reproduction. Stay away from off-white, ivory, or cream colored papers. These may be fine for "exhibition" print purposes but are really not the best for graphic reproduction.

The character of photographic paper surfaces also influences the brilliance and detail of a print. The more textured and duller the surface, the less detail and brilliance will be obtained from the negative. Matte surface prints make poor copy for any reproduction process.

Photographers' tricks in the darkroom? A good photographer has "a bag full." And as one excellent photographer puts it, "I'm not talking, but I use them every day."

Basic Facts

Chapter 5

WAYS TO PROTECT PHOTOGRAPHS

Almost on a weekly basis I receive photographs in the mail from someone who wants to sell something. That is not unusual, but what is absolutely startling is the number of photographs that are fastened together with either a staple or a paper clip.

Next are those prints or slides that are not "backed" at all, a single thin glossy print in an equally thin envelope. To make matters worse, some of the envelopes are neatly folded with the rest of the mail, and a rubber band around the entire pack.

Most of the photographs are from manufacturing firms in the graphic arts and allied industries. The computer industry is following quickly with this bad habit. I pity the editor of a trade magazine who needs to use a bad print in his next issue.

Sure, time is of the essence, and the mail, regardless of increasing postage rates, is not reaching its destination any faster. A damaged print or slide has no value to anyone, even if it is delivered on time.

Valuable time is lost because someone has not packaged a photograph properly. Do not count on the safety of a bubble-type mailing envelope. Always use a heavy cardboard in the envelope and if possible cross-grain the board. It may cost a little more on postage but a good photograph deserves to travel first class without the possibility of damage.

WAYS TO PROTECT PHOTOGRAPHS

There is a relatively new problem which is caused by the extensive use of laser printers and copiers for cover letters, resumes, and news releases. Some of these machines do not fuse the image, printed words, "tightly" enough to the paper. We have seen several cases where the printed words did not adhere properly. When this comes in contact with a white area of a photograph, a definite "lift-off" occurs. A good protection is to fasten a greaseless overlay sheet to the photograph.

The following tips are quick and easy to follow, and can be used in the mail room or by anyone who handles photographs for reproduction purposes. A little care makes a world of difference.

PAPER CLIPS should never be used on photographs. The emulsion of a print is soft, and the mark left by the paper clip will show up in the printing operation. This mark may then require some costly retouching.

RUBBER STAMPS do not ordinarily damage the back of a print. However, the wooden block is sometimes tilted in the stamping operation and this marking may show through the front of the print. Also rubber stamping ink does not dry quickly and smearing may occur if prints are stacked one on top of the other after stamping. This type of ink may "bleed" through the photographic paper.

ROLLING of prints (if you must) should be done with the picture surface on the outside. If the emulsion should develop a slight cracking, it will close up when the print is laid flat. It is best to avoid this problem by shipping prints flat.

OILY OVERLAYS such as draftsmen's tracing paper or commercial wax paper should not come in direct contact with the front of a print's surface. The heat of a hand or finger can melt some of the oily particles of this type of material and can easily ruin a retouched print.

MAILING WITHOUT a sturdy backing can be dangerous to prints or slides. The mere marking of "DO NOT FOLD" is not enough. It is actually necessary to make it impossible to fold a package that contains prints. Caution: Some standard mailers, even if bought from the post office, are too thin. Double thick chipboard on both sides of a print is a safer method.

FACE TO FACE mailing or handling of prints should be avoided. Dirt particles may get in between and ruin not only one print but it can ruin two at the same time.

FINGERPRINTS should be relegated to the FBI. Airbrushing work on a print can be completely ruined with a fingerprint. We have actually seen a fingerprint in a photograph in an annual report.

The suggestions in this article may appear basic. They are. It is because basics are allowed to slip by that problems occur.

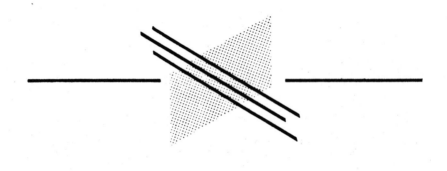

Basic Facts   *Chapter 6*

PERIODS AND HYPHENS
MISS THE ! MARK

It won't be easy to change a habit that we've been using for years and years. No one seems to know where it all started, that is the use of periods and hyphens in advertising. There are, of course, some very valid reasons to use these punctuation marks. Our language could not exist without them, AND THERE ARE PROPER TIMES FOR THEIR USE. The issue is really not about the use of these two marks, but rather their MISUSE.

THE PROBLEM ACTUALLY centers around one word, "READABILITY," and what effect these two punctuation marks have on the reader, regardless of whether the media is text, advertisements or even television.

Now we all agree that a period means to STOP, that it is the end of something. We've all learned that in school, and, we are not suggesting that it be changed, EXCEPT in advertising headlines.

A period means to stop and take a break, however short, and then continue reading. Seven out of ten headlines used in advertising use a period after five words or even as few as one word. What does this period do for the reader of THIS headline? It TELLS THEM to stop.

Now according to the best of ad men, STOPPING is the very last

PERIODS AND HYPHENS

thing that the copywriter has in mind, yet that is exactly what his period IS DOING.

For example, take the headline, "YOU TOO SHOULD BUY OUR PRODUCT." Now if we split this into two lines and insert a period, the copy now reads,

YOU TOO.
SHOULD BUY OUR PRODUCT.

Since the period is not an emphasizing mark, it makes the reader stop. It would be far better if an exclamation mark were used:

YOU TOO!
SHOULD BUY OUR PRODUCT!

Now don't blame the printer! The printer will reproduce what the copywriter or the artist gives to him! Printers rarely make changes in "camera ready" copy unless it is a very blatant or obvious mistake, and even then the printer usually checks since the error may be intentional to get reader attention. Let's take this use of the period just one step further.

Let's find out what one of the leading writers of advertising copy has to say about periods in headlines.

As reported in ADWEEK, David Ogilvy (of Ogilvy and Mather) calls it as he sees it. "Headlines," he warns, "should never have periods which STOP the readers dead in their tracks." Mr. Ogilvy is not alone in feeling that considerable loss of understanding of typography occurs in the advertising field.

If a copywriter really wants to emphasize a word or even an entire sentence, what is he to use? Try the exclamation mark for emphasis. It does wonders to pump up a word or statement.

Old fashioned? NO WAY! This powerful mark is more usable

PERIODS AND HYPHENS

today than it has ever been. However, I must add a note of caution about the use of this handy mark. Don't use it for a simple statement such as, "It was a beautiful day." Change the copy to read, "What a beautiful day it was!" Now you have the punch you can feel.

Try this with just a one-word headline for a state publicity ad. ARIZONA. The period makes the reader stop, with no emphasis on the word. Now, try ARIZONA! Wow, I want to read on and maybe I'll even go there. That is the message you intended for the reader right from the start. The exclamation mark is a super tool for emphasis which can be used in many advertising headlines, but unfortunately it is not.

William Strunk, Jr., in his book, THE ELEMENTS OF STYLE, states emphatically, "Omit a period after a title or a heading." So much for the "period."

Oh yes, the HYPHEN. This is one of the most overused and MISUSED punctuation marks on the typewriter, typesetting machine or computer keyboard that has ever been invented. Of course it is useful and there are thousands of words that must be hyphenated. These words are NOT in question here. Even at the end of a line in text, when push comes to shove, use a hyphen. Sometimes there is just no other way. But never, never have hyphens appear at the end of three or more successive lines. Some editing should be done in these cases.

Let's consider the "newer" method of ragged right-hand typesetting. It's the "in way," like it or not. The hyphen, like the period, is supposed to make the reader do something and it does. The reader doesn't really stop, as with the period, but rather he gropes for the rest of the word. If the word is on the next line, well, that's basically easy to handle. Though on a long line of type, say six inches, a reader may very well need to go back to the beginning of the hyphenated word to make the "connection." If the hyphen were not there at all, the word would be more meaningful and

PERIODS AND HYPHENS

certainly more readable, and isn't readability the reason for putting words on paper?

Look at this example. In a very prestigious annual report with ragged right-hand typesetting three inches wide, set in 10 point Century typestyle, there were nineteen hyphens in eleven inches of text. This is stretching the use of hyphens and the readers' eyes a bit too far. It's just plain hard to read. Add a small word, take out a small word, change a word without changing the meaning, that's how to eliminate many hyphens.

In another annual report, with two columns to a page, a word was separated by a hyphen (COR-) at the end of page four (left hand page). On the facing page was a full-page photograph, and so were THE NEXT TWO PAGES. The end of the hyphenated word (PORATION) finally appeared on top of page eight first column. The word was CORPORATION. It's not funny when it's true.

What are the basic problems with periods and hyphens in typography? Remember that READABILITY is the key word in any form of advertising. It makes little difference if the ad is for a product or a type of service and if it appears in a magazine, a newspaper or on television. It is human nature to gloss over something that is not easy to read. Take it from the experts in advertising, MAKE IT READABLE OR THE PUBLIC WON'T BUY WHATEVER IT IS THAT YOU ARE TRYING TO SELL. And that is a FACT!

Basic Facts

Chapter 7

OUT OF REGISTER, WHITE LETTERS

In four-color printing, if the reverse (white) letters in ads or other areas are not 100% clear white, then the visible printing is out of register! This is a FACT, not FICTION. To prove the point, take a 10 power magnifying glass and look at the dot pattern, or along the straight line of a white letter.

Many ads do not require type to be run in four colors. Single color or even multicolors in a line (not halftone) version lend themselves just fine for white letters, so why complicate the problems?

Virtually no magazine can give you a clean purple color with one impression, unless you are willing to pay for the extra expense of running a separate color cylinder.

The problem is not with the purple color or any other color. The problem is that when small type is run in reverse using multicolors, there is a good possibility of having out-of-register printing.

Many ads that are run in the basic four colors do have reverse letters somewhere in the ad. For the most part, this is at the bottom of the ad in the address or telephone area, an area that MUST be readable.

OUT OF REGISTER, WHITE LETTERS

One way to solve this problem is to run only 12-point or larger type in white letters. If an under-color is required to get some sheen in the reverse letter area, use only the yellow printing plate to get this effect. If it is slightly out of register, yellow is not as noticeable since the human eye does not perceive yellow as well. This yellow might well be in the form of a 10% screen which will, under black, produce a sheen.

Another problem with white letters is that the designer will use a mottled background made up from yellow, blue and black. If small white letters are introduced in this design, the printing will be nearly impossible to read.

Another problem occurs when the designer introduces an overall 10% black screen over a block of type. The white letters will give a foggy appearance similar to looking through dirty or spotted glasses.

Registration problems can develop on a printed page at any place where colors either join or are printed one over the other. Printing presses, especially the web type, are not 100% perfect when it comes to register. Even when the art work is prepared for exact register, most presses have a problem holding register at high speed. There are other factors that come into play beside the presses themselves. Paper can and does stretch vertically, and it also can shift horizontally on the press. The slightest movement will be seen in reverse letters which use multicolors in design.

One solution to this out-of-register problem is the art of trapping. This can be done by slightly over and under exposing the film during the color separation process. This choking or spreading can be done so that the printed letters either butt or overlap as needed.

An old problem often surfaces in this modern way of preparing copy for a printer. Separate boards of copy, each having a different color, will be presented to a client. He is told that when all of

OUT OF REGISTER, WHITE LETTERS

the colors are printed, one over the other, his ad or job will look great.

Preparing art and final negatives for printing multicolor work is not a new idea. It has been around for more than 75 years. The issue is that designers don't take advantage of a very simple system.

A red over a yellow with the red being slightly out of register will be hardly noticeable. But if a blue over yellow is out of register, the result will not be a clean green. Even with a press color proof there is no guarantee that all colors will register at high speed. They will register if the artwork is prepared using the trapping technique.

It is a fallacy to think that, even if three colors are out of register, the black printer will cover the problem and all will be well. True, the black printer will make its own white letter, however, the other colors which are not in register, also will appear in the black letter. The result is an unreadable letter or paragraph, and certainly not a clean white letter.

White letters can be most effective when properly used. The knowledge of the designer of the printed job is the key to readability.

GRAY AND BLACK OUT OF REGISTER

Basic Facts

Chapter 8

BORDERS, RULES AND DOTS

Every punctuation mark has a reason to exist and every one performs a specific task. When are they misused? When it comes to advertising, EVERY DAY OF THE WEEK AND TWICE ON SUNDAY!

Borders around ads or around a block of type in an ad are not punctuation marks. But they are used in the same manner. They are designed to create emphasis or importance.

Borders, rules and dots (periods), and exclamation marks can become a very effective tool in an ad. That is, when they are used properly. Designers for some of the most expensive ads in the most prodigious magazines pay little attention to using these marks correctly.

It is difficult, in a book such as this, without a visual drawing, to point out some of the problems of design. Let your imagination take over.

Picture an undertaker's ad, 6"x6" in a newspaper or a magazine, with a 1/4" solid black border around it. Horrible! It would be better to use a parallel 2 point border. This type of an ad requires dignity, not an illusion of a hearse.

At Christmas time, a holly border signifies the spirit of the season. This type of border is not the best for a July picnic type of

BORDERS, RULES AND DOTS

ad. The selection of a border, if one is to be used, does require some thinking. Seasonal ad borders are generally in good taste. With the myriad of borders available in all types of typographic media, choosing an appropriate design should be easy.

An "over use" of rules, just to call the reader's attention, is totally worthless. Picture a 8"x10" ad, without any illustrations. This ad had four blocks of type, each with a 6-point black solid border around them.

The only thing that the reader sees when looking at this ad is black borders. The message in the type is lost, and the ad does not do what was intended. Redesign the ad. Keep the rules out and design a better visual approach.

Dots, or periods, have found their way in much modern advertising. Most all headlines, even if only one word, carry a period. What does this period do for the headline? Nothing! Oh, yes, it surely does something! It makes the reader stop. In advertising, stopping the reader is the very last thing that an ad should do. That is, at the headline. Let the reader go to the sales message WITHOUT STOPPING.

At the end of a sentence, yes, use a period, but not before. There are other marks that can be used in a one word headline. Use an exclamation mark! Emphasize the word. Sell the message!

Punctuation in advertising can be as effective as the entire sales message. Tie this in with an appropriate border and you will have an ad that will get attention. Of course there are many ads, because of a particular design, that do not require a border.

One of the problems, and there are many, is that the creative spirit of the designer of an ad has been let out of the cage. True, let's not go back to the days of the "Keystone Cops" when the word creativity did not exist.

Be creative, yes, but consider two important elements. Design and the reader. If the design is not geared to the reader, then the reader will not buy whatever the ad is trying to sell.

CREATIVE FREEDOM is a must, otherwise being in this business would surely be boredom. Yet this freedom should be tempered with a more than average knowledge of the printing industry. This is especially so when our computer age offers almost limitless possibilities in the area of design.

In designing, care must be exercised when an ad is created that uses multiple colors. Computerized design using hundreds of colors may look appealing, but remember that a printer uses four basic colors.

True, with overprinting and the use of screen tints of the four colors a printer can come up with a great many variations of the basic colors. Yet the end result may not match the computerized color since many of these colors are not printable.

If a special color is desired, such as a metallic color, be prepared to pay for an extra run (or plate) charge. Color swatches are a big help and the inks are generally available, yet an exact match may not result. Paper texture and the color of the paper needs to be considered. It is advisable to have a "draw down" of the ink on the actual paper that will be used.

In the final analysis, "think about the result" while you are creating.

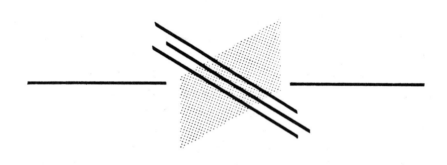

Basic Facts

Chapter 9

PRODUCING ANNUAL REPORTS

There should be little difficulty in putting down on paper, the facts of an annual report. In the broadest sense you are dealing with facts such as a financial report, photographs and the basic story of your institution, commercial company and dozens of columns of people's names and even more, many pages of related figures.

If all of this material is handed to you, what then is the problem? The problem is that no one has handed you a DESIGN. It is impossible to place all of this material in proper order unless a design is first established.

The predominant use of annual reports is by industries followed by colleges and schools, hospitals, philanthropic groups, legal groups, churches, and the list goes on and on. Profit or nonprofit, it makes little difference. Annual reports are a must.

Some annual reports go into great detail regarding the financial section. Investors and philanthropists take a good look at this section.

Some annual reports do not have a financial report section. They prefer to issue a list of donors or the names of individuals that have set up a type of scholarship or special awards program.

PRODUCING ANNUAL REPORTS

Sounds simple enough. All you need to do is go to a typewriter or computer, punch a few keys and in no time you have material that will go to the printing department with a basket full of typed sheets. Now this basket contains not only typed sheets. There are many loose photographs with the legend or name securely fastened with a staple. And then there is the note to the printer, "just use your best judgement, I'll be back in a month or so."

Now, if you think this is funny, it is not. And if you think that this does not happen, you are wrong. It does!

The reason that this situation happens is simple and factual. Many of the persons who have a direct responsibility for the production of an annual report have not had the proper training.

Here is a hint. Do you know, really, what you need to know about such items as: DESIGN: MARGINS AND BLEEDS, PRINTING PAPERS AND THEIR SURFACE FINISHES, INK COLORS WITH SOME OF THEIR PROBLEMS, TYPE STYLES (WHICH TO AVOID), PHOTOGRAPHS AND THEIR SCREENING, DUOTONES (WHAT THEY ARE), BEST BINDING METHODS FOR REPORTS, MAILING AND POSTAL REQUIREMENTS, and there are more.

Yes, all of these items go into the making of an annual report. In most cases these items are just as important as the financial report. If the overall report is poorly presented, it has a direct bearing on the reader of the financial report.

Before we look at some annual reports, there is one more crucial factor. Who is preparing the report? If there is only one person preparing the report, he had better have three or four people who can offer advice or possibly an unbiased critique. An "it looks good to me" answer is not what is really needed. This will only get you and the report in trouble.

TO OFFER A CRITIQUE MEANS TO COME UP WITH A

BETTER ALTERNATIVE IDEA. IT DOES NOT MEAN TO CRITICIZE.

Now, let's look at a group of 25 annual reports and see how they might be changed.

DESIGN

All of the 25 reports we critiqued were lacking in some areas of design. The cover design was poor, the text position had no style in spacing, photographs were poorly cropped, type styles and size were bad, and it goes on, as we shall see.

Several reports appeared to have the text clipped from a newspaper and actually used as copy to be printed. One report used line spacing similar to what we used in grade school, very wide. One report featured a "plea for funds." We might have sent a donation but there was no address in the entire report.

It is not easy to design an annual report. Every year, even if the same designer is used, he tries to come up with something new. And this is truly a problem. Where does one get fresh ideas? Try this: every year the WALL STREET JOURNAL and the NEW YORK TIMES issue a list of companies that offer their annual report, free. Get them, look at them, study them. Copy their design? NO! Get ideas? YES!

Several reports used one inch, solid, bars running from top to bottom on eight successive pages. It is virtually impossible to have these bars look uniform in color. The solid bars we critiqued looked more like a swatch card from an ink company showing what SHADES of a particular color are available.

If you want a side color bar on a particular page as a design factor of the report, use a 40% screen of only one color. Never use two screened colors, one over the other, in an attempt to create still another color. If you do, be prepared for a color variation.

SIZE AND NUMBER OF PAGES

In the reports we reviewed, the trimmed size varied from 6 3/4" x 10 1/2" to 8 1/2" x 11 1/2". Most were in the "standard" range of 8 1/2" by 11". The number of pages also varied from 8 pages to 72 pages. The average report was 32 pages.

It is virtually impossible to determine the number of pages for a report at the outset, unless there is a history of the number of pages over the years. Archives are helpful although not a guarantee. You may find that a particular executive this year wants a full page photograph. A good guide to creating a successful report is to prepare paper dummies in 4 and 8 page sections. This will ease the problem of eliminating or adding single pages as you create the rough layout.

COVER

"You can't tell a book by its cover." Not true when it comes to annual reports. Generally, a cover carries a theme, either a date, a logo, a photograph or even a slogan. Wise men claim that the less copy there is on a cover, the better. Many industrial types of annual report covers carry only a logo, leaving the features for the text.

Five of the reports carried a photograph, while 20 used only type. The designers that used photographs did not take the texture of the cover paper into consideration. The printed result was not good. If photographs are to be considered, then consider a glossy stock. If a stock is to be embossed, there are many paper surfaces that will give an excellent result. This is true for heat foil or blind embossing.

INSIDE PAPER

All paper does not PRINT the same even though it may look or feel the same. Standard machine coated, high gloss coated, smooth antique, standard antique, all of these papers accept ink differently. And all require that photographic negatives be shot differently, where contrast and appearance are concerned.

Even type styles are affected by the texture of the paper. Our critique found that four reports used an antique finish paper. The photographs came out poorly. There was no contrast in them at all. Had the photographs been printed on a coated stock the result would have been much better.

Several reports used an ivory coated paper. The result was pleasing to the eye. This also helped some over contrasted photographs.

INK

There are "tricks of the trade" that can be used with much printed work. However, when it comes to annual reports it is better to stay with the basics. Yes, you can use a multitude of colors, screen colors or blocks of solids. Yet there should be only one objective: a good, clean, readable report without going into a kaleidoscope of colors for the sake of getting attention.

Designers will experiment with wanting to make a "special color" by screening a blue over a yellow, or by using a blue over a red screen. To make matters worse, they then attempt to have small white, (reverse) letters appear in that screen pattern. The result is that the type is not readable.

Several reports used the DUOTONE screening process with excellent results. (See Duotone under photographs).

PHOTOGRAPHS

Perhaps the most troublesome job in working with annual reports is "the CARE and FEEDING of photographs." Yes, photographs should be handled as though they were "ALIVE."

Reasons photographs in a report can look so bad are: they may have bent ears, a crease down the middle, notes attached to the photos with staples or, are written on the back with ink that bled through. Another common problem is poor storage, such as, using photos that laid for years in "grandfather's trunk."

It is impossible to critique photographs when any of the above occurs. Thirteen of the 25 reports had poor to very poor photographs. It is a sure bet that some of the above was the reason.

Printers cannot make good copy from a bad print. There are photo studios that can be of help. Use them if it will improve the photo. In working with photographs, get an early start so that you may have time for a remake.

DUOTONES

Here is an excellent way of enhancing most any photograph. Of course you will need a compatible second ink color and a second press run. A Duotone is made from 2 sets of screened negatives of the same photograph. Two screen angles are used, one at 45 degrees, the other at 75 degrees. Pages 7:56 and 7:57 of the Lithographers Manual, 8th edition 1988, describe the process in greater detail.

When using Duotone second colors, it is possible to use a side bar in one of these colors. It gives the report a good two color effect.

TYPE

Some of the 25 reports had a problem with type. In most instances it was the result of the type style (typeface) choice. Other problems were line spacing, type size and use of hyphens. One report used seven hyphens in a nine inch column of right-hand ragged copy. A benefit of right-hand ragged typography is to avoid hyphens.

Runover hyphenated words from the bottom of a page to the top of the next page should be avoided. Even hyphenated words going to the top of the next column are not desirable. Changing a word, or adding a three letter word can, in most cases, control this problem.

A Bodoni type face style, printed on textured paper is hard to read. This is especially so when the reading lines are wide, such as eight inches. There are many other, and often more readable, text type faces to choose from, such as Times Roman, Optima, Century Textbook, or Bookman. These appear to lead the preference fields.

Annual reports are not designed to be newspaper ads. We have seen annual reports using 36 point letters in headlines. Dignity is a word that fits the type style of an annual report.

BINDING

The newer type of binding, "perfect binding," is not generally suitable for annual reports. The reason? When the report is opened it does not lie flat. There are now newer patented "perfect binding" methods that overcome this problem to a great extent. Binding for annual reports is best when the time tested, two-staple method is used. THE TOTAL NUMBER OF INSIDE PAGES AND THE TYPE OF COVER HAVE A DIRECT BEARING ON THE BINDING METHOD.

Spiral binding or other types of mechanical binding methods are not as appealing for reports. We have seen some plastic bound reports that were acceptable. However, these did have a "sales promotion" type of appearance to them.

MAILING/SHIPPING

Perhaps the most important issue of handling the finished annual report is that of shipping. The cost of postage is a constant factor.

The outside envelope must be considered along with the actual size of the report. An oversize envelope can cost extra postage.

The material of which the envelope is made is important. The "no-tear" envelope is great, but it is expensive. The standard brown envelope sometimes comes to the recipient with part of a corner ripped open. The postmaster will tell you to "use a box." That's more postage. The best mailer appears to be a "Jiffy" envelope or one of the bubble pack series. Mailing should be considered in the DESIGN stage. It might be possible to use a lighter weight stock in order to qualify for a lower postage rate.

The random selection of the 25 annual reports used in our critique points out that THERE IS an area where improvement is desirable.

Basic Facts — Chapter 10

BINDING PERFECT BOUND BOOKS

Skill in designing printing and advertising may not be getting all the respect that it deserves. The word "design" is treated much too lightly when various printing items are formulated. Designing is not simply a matter of setting type by any method and pasting some proofs on a board. Placing a few blue guidelines does not qualify as design. Type sizes and styles, binding margins, kind of binding, position of type and photographs or illustrations are just a few items that must be taken into consideration in production of proper layout and design.

Following are some areas that can cause problems in coming up with an acceptable final product.

A 7 1/2"x10" ad with a complete border, bound into a magazine size 8"x10 3/4", will have a problem along the binding edge. The ad text or the borders of an ad should not be wider than 7" to allow a full 1/2" white margin at the binding edge. Using the 7 1/2" width allows only a 1/4" white space on each side, and this is too small a margin for perfect binding. It must be remembered that perfect bound magazines, books or annual reports do not open like pages in a three-ring binder.

Full bleed pages, including those with a one-point border all around, should also have a full 1/2" blank area at the binding margin. Even if the art work calls for the design to run into the binding margin, the text must remain at least 1/2" from the binding margin.

Another common problem is that many ads and text are designed for a specific magazine and without any size revision, are then sent to another magazine that may have DIFFERENT margin requirements. Once such an ad or text is released to another publication, it may be too late to make any changes.

This same principle is true for text that has a 1/2" margin allocated to go around the ad. While the 1/2" space has been allowed at the binding margin, this amount is generally barely enough. In perfect binding as much as 1/16" can be trimmed off at the binding margin for "roughing," leaving only 7/16" margin which is hardly enough when the magazine is glued and bound.

Binding margins must be carefully considered when making the initial size layout. Type that runs across the binding margin should have sufficient space allocated so that the letters are not bound in the magazine. There is a safe way to determine this space: Have the binder advise you exactly how much trim is to be taken off the magazine or annual report at the binding edge.

In designing a double spread for perfect bound magazines, it is wrong to simply cut the art work in the center with a razor blade. Too little margin and a full letter may be lost in binding. As well, an excessive margin will give the appearance of two words. Binding margins must be considered carefully when making the initial size layout; this is especially true when large letters, such as 36-point, are used to run across a spread.

IT IS IMPORTANT TO CONSIDER BOTH THE NUMBER OF PAGES AND THE OVERALL THICKNESS OF A PUBLICATION WHEN DESIGNING ART THAT CROSSES A BINDING MARGIN.

Folders or brochures glued into a magazine deserve special attention. "Removable" glue strips are generally applied 3/8" from the binding edge. This spacing suggests that an ad or text on the following page, "underneath" such an insert, must have an additional margin at the binding edge. A full 3/4" is suggested. If this is not a consideration, then the glue strip will be directly on the text edge of the underneath ad and make it unreadable.

The equipment which applies the amount of glue (adhesive) that is distributed to each copy of a publication must be carefully monitored.

If too much glue is applied, the "squeeze" action of the equipment will force some of the glue beyond the binding edge. This will adhere to the succeeding sheets and make them difficult to turn. It is also quite possible that this excess glue will creep into the text area of the pages.

Some inserts have a separate 3/4" perforated strip stapled or glued to the insert at the binding edge. This is a separate bindery operation, a perforation that permits removal of the insert without tearing any pages.

Single reply cards should be perforated at no more than 3/8" from the binding edge. The stub should not protrude into the magazine; if it does, the next few pages will be difficult to turn and may cause an annoyance to the reader.

ILLUSTRATION: BINDING MARGINS

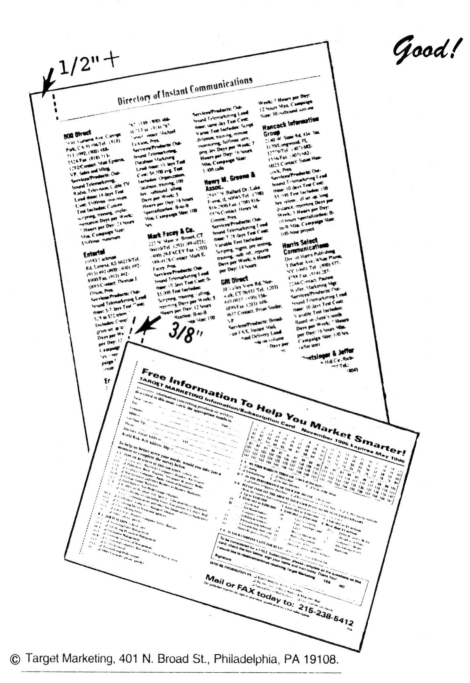

© Target Marketing, 401 N. Broad St., Philadelphia, PA 19108.

Basic Facts

Chapter 11

TRADE SHOW ADVERTISING EXHIBITS VS PUBLICATION ADS

The answer to "which is better" is not easy to understand nor is it predictable. There are many factors that must first be considered.

Trade magazines do, very definitely, exhibit at trade shows. This indicates these magazines realize there is a value in being in trade shows. What is the value? To meet and greet the exhibitors at these shows in order to sell advertising space.

And why are manufacturers and suppliers at trade shows? To impart information about their products and services and to SELL! Both groups are at trade shows for a very honest, legitimate purpose: MORE BUSINESS!

The question of exhibiting at a trade show versus magazine advertising may again be a standoff. That is, choosing one OR the other.

What needs to be analyzed is this: HOW MUCH OF EITHER DOES A COMPANY NEED TO DO TO EXIST? This question, now, becomes one for individual company research. Millions, yes, millions of dollars are spent annually on this research. Some companies find the right answer while others wind up in chapter 11.

Past and present dollars spent in both media come into play. Of course company profit and loss factors are also vital factors. Add to this the size, attendance and calendar dates of a show versus the size, the cost, the number of insertions and circulation of ads and you wind up with the puzzle.

Then, to make the issue more complicated, add in the location of a show. Will there be competing shows in the same month? Or worse yet, in the same geographical area? An ad in a magazine does not have that problem.

An exhibit by a large exhibitor taking 5000 square feet of space will draw a crowd, with proper merchandising of course. Yet, a company with only 300 square feet of space may draw all the people that it can handle. Proper merchandising is the key in both cases.

Obviously, a 5000 square foot exhibit, considering the cost of the space, sales manpower, in and out and setup cost, as well as lodging plus a myriad of incidental costs can be enormous. It is most important for an exhibitor to advertise that his firm will be in a certain trade show. This dollar amount can be staggering if a firm advertises with full page ads in five or six national publications. Being in a trade show can be expensive.

There is little question that early and proper advertising is needed to draw a crowd. A new invention or an improved system can be of real help. The most widely read trade magazines do have the greatest number of full page ads. However, a smaller regional or a specific audience oriented type of magazine can be just as beneficial with a one-half page ad providing that the ad is well designed. The geographical market area may be the determining factor.

The magazine that is moved from the president's desk down to the shop supervisory level or even to the company lunchroom has real value. Many an employee's idea for an equipment change or an operating change has proven very beneficial to a company. Ads do call attention to a company and their product or service.

When advertising in a trade magazine, serious consideration should be given to the number of issues in which an ad is to appear. Generally, a "one-shot" ad will not be remembered very long. Exposure to a reader is essential for both the trade magazine advertiser or trade show exhibitor.

For example, a trade show may generate an attendance of 30,000 bona-fide registrants (exhibitors excluded). A trade magazine may have a circulation of 80,000. Is one better than the other because the numbers are different? Not really. The question of numbers must be taken with a grain of salt, or aspirin.

Many orders are written up at a trade show because of eyeball to eyeball sales contact. With a trade magazine a lead must be followed up in one form or another to get the order.

At a trade show, a potential buyer can, in many cases, see a piece of equipment in actual operation. To get the same result from an advertisement it may require a visit to a plant or a manufacturer's factory to see how a piece of equipment operates.

Does the question of what to do, trade shows or trade advertisement, come down to pure dollars and cents? Maybe a budget of some type? It can. However a more detailed analysis should govern any expenditure. Past experience, perhaps over a five year period, is a good way to start. Compare every known factor for both methods. From sales costs to markup to profit.

Then, set your goal. Where does your company want to be in the next five years? Do you have a solid marketing plan? And lest we forget, a marketing plan is not the same as a sales plan or an advertising plan.

It is quite possible that the power of advertising and the exposure at a trade show will mesh hand in hand to get the business you set for your goal.

The author has been in printing, advertising and trade show management for over 50 years. And, my answer to the basic question is that BOTH trade advertising and trade show exhibits have a definite place to get that, sometimes elusive, signature on the dotted line.

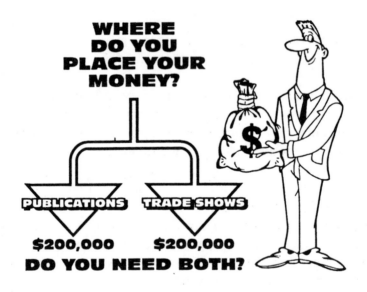

Basic Facts

Chapter 12

UPGRADING NEWSPAPER ADS

SHOULD NEWSPAPERS GET INVOLVED IN DESIGN AND TYPOGRAPHY FOR THEIR CONSUMER AD CLIENTS? YES! And most all newspapers have a display ad department that can and does not only get involved, but it's part of the price of an ad. The question then comes down to one basic factor. WHY ARE SO MANY ADS NOT READABLE, EITHER THROUGH POOR DESIGN OR BAD TYPOGRAPHY?

Ever since newspapers started using a fine halftone screen, such as a 133 line, up from the traditional 85 line, halftones have become darker and darker. In fact, some faces of models featuring clothing, both men and women, look more like an oval smudge. Then, too, those terrible 6-point reverse letters set in a Ultra Bodoni typeface are impossible to read.

WHAT CAUSES THESE PROBLEMS?

Is it a lack of knowledge by the person who takes the ad from the client and just passes it along for production?

Is it the "camera ready" concept where some newspapers and magazines offer a discount for that type of copy?

Is it the typesetter/computer operator of the newspaper who "composes" the ad?

UPGRADING NEWSPAPER ADS

The answers to each of these questions is "YES." These are all real problems. There is one way to start eliminating these problems and that is to acknowledge that these are indeed problems.

What department is the most likely to be of help in correcting these problems? Most newspapers have three basic departments: one, is the editorial or news department; second, is the circulation department, and then there is the advertising department, without whom no newspaper can exist.

It does appear that we can, at least, pin this basic problem down to one department. Advertising. Having said this, it is now necessary to break down the advertising department into the three issues of complaint. And this will not be easy. Let's take them one at a time and develop some answers.

Is it a lack of knowledge? YES. A secretary who has been upgraded to the advertising department and now takes "off-the-street" ads does not have the experience to discuss an ad with a client. She does not really know how an ad will look after it is printed until she reads the newspaper. And even then she may not be able to offer a sound critique.

Can she suggest to a client that she should leave out the overall screen? Can she suggest that a solid 12 point border is not even good for a funeral director's ad? Of course not, but why not? If she were trained in typography and had some schooling in design, she not only would be well qualified, she would be a real asset to the newspaper.

CAMERA READY also can be described as CAMERA WRONG. Take any ad, let's say it's a six-inch square ad of nothing but type and some type at the bottom is in 6-point. It all looks good on a proof. But then the client produces a screen tint which he wants over the entire ad, 100 line screen. This example is NOT CAMERA READY art.

TRAINING! Show the employees who accept "camera ready"

UPGRADING NEWSPAPER ADS

art what CAN happen with certain types of customer-prepared art. Have a file on hand of some "POOR" ads for the customer to examine.

In an effort to be creative, in both magazine and newspaper ads, a BASIC DESIGN feature is being misused. Flat screen tints ranging from 65 lines to 100 lines should not be used over some type faces.

The paramount reason for good ad design is READABILITY. This was true in the thirties and it is still true in the nineties. "If they can't read the ad, chances are they won't buy the product or service."

Modern technology will not solve this problem. It takes know-how and a real "feel" of how a screened area will reproduce on a press. There are many guides available showing screen values ranging from 5% to 50% of various "line" screens.

Is it in the composing/computer room? YES!

If an ad is brought in and a REVERSE PANEL is marked for Ultra Bodoni or a strong serifed type face, SCREAM! For most reverses, a gothic or other sans serif typeface is needed. 8-point or larger is suggested.

Now we all know that newspaper deadlines are like few others. The composing/computer room operator must have two items on his mind. The first, he must have the knowledge about what to change and, second, he must have the authority to make such a change. AUTHORITY? This may never happen.

All production people are a part of the involvement to see that an ad can be read. READABILITY SELLS PRODUCTS AND SERVICES! From the account salesman to the pressman, every ad, and, for that matter, the entire newspaper, MUST BE READABLE.

This is the paramount reason for IN-PLANT TRAINING.

UPGRADING NEWSPAPER ADS

HALF PRICE 2 DAYS ONLY

EVERY PIECE OF FURNITURE
IN OUR STOCK
SOFAS, TABLES, LAMPS, CHAIRS
COMPLETE ROOMS

*

WE WILL DELIVER IN 24 HOURS

*

THE FURNITURE STORE
921 STIRLING AVE, NE, BROWERTON

HALF PRICE 2 DAYS ONLY

EVERY PIECE OF FURNITURE
IN OUR STOCK
SOFAS, TABLES, LAMPS, CHAIRS
COMPLETE ROOMS

*

WE WILL DELIVER IN 24 HOURS

*

THE FURNITURE STORE
921 STIRLING AVE, NE, BROWERTON

Many factors enter into the choice of a type face besides legibility. One of the most important is weight or color. Some faces print light and some print dark; between the extremes of very

Vogue Bold Italic, l.

Many factors enter into the choice of a type face besides legibility. One of the most important is weight or color. Some faces print light and some print dark; be-

Bodoni Bold Italic, l.

Many factors enter into the choice of a type face besides legibility. One of the most important is weight or color. Some faces print light and some print dark;

Futura Bold, l.

Many factors enter into the choice of a type face besides legibility. One of the most important is weight or color. Some faces print

Ultra Bodoni, li.

ALL OF THESE EXAMPLES SHOW THAT A LIGHTER SCREEN SHOULD BE USED

UPGRADING NEWSPAPER ADS

GOOD USE OF

SCREENS

Call Advertising Age, Talk to your Classified Representative, and Get Results! Phone 1-800-955-5562, or 1-800-925-5562

Advertising Age.
IT'S ALL ABOUT MARKETING

LORRAINE KULICK
EXECUTIVE DIRECTOR
N.J.S.A.C.O.P.
777 ALEXANDER ROAD, SUITE 203
PRINCETON, NEW JERSEY 08540-6325

TELE: 609/452-0014   FAX: 609/452-1893

UPGRADING NEWSPAPER ADS

Many newspapers ads, especially the two column by six to eight inches deep are poorly designed. In many cases too much copy is squeezed into this space. Auction notices and special sale notices are notorious for this problem.

Granted, advertising space costs money. Yet if a reader can't read the message then the cost of the ad is meaningless. It will not bring results. GOOD DESIGN CAN HELP! It is important to get the attention of the reader.

THE AUCTION AD BELOW GETS YOUR ATTENTION. IT IS A <u>WELL DESIGNED AD</u>. (Reduced to fit space)

Basic Facts

Chapter 13

DIRECT DIGITAL COLOR SEPARATION

There is little, if any, question that computerized direct digital color separation is the most modern method for making color separations for all types of input from computer art, RGB scans and digital cameras.

Today it is unusual to find an ad agency without a computer. Page layout and composition have all but disappeared as a hand operation. Increasingly artists are turning to the computer in ways never known just a few years ago. This is true not only for page layout and composition, but also for artwork.

The artist can now "scan in" flat copy or transparencies, combine these images with text and have a color hard copy comp in no time using a desktop color printer. The colors will not be of reproduction quality, but will offer the client a good idea of how his ad will appear, all in a fraction of time.

Today, 24 bit color boards yielding 16 million colors, are common with most computers today. Several excellent computer drawing programs, newer and better image editing programs, have been introduced each with enhanced capabilities. All are positive steps toward making the printing industry a near total digital industry.

DIRECT DIGITAL COLOR SEPARATIONS

The weakest link in the desk top revolution is the color correction problem and the linking between personal computers and quality output devices.

Recently, there has been an influx of new, less expensive scanners on the market for the computer desktop publisher. This has made it a great deal easier for the computer enthusiast to get quality pictures into his computer. It opens vast new markets for the commercial computer artist and graphic designer.

However, there is a word of caution. With these new scanners, some think that if "I cannot make accurate color corrections on my computer, then maybe I can compensate for this anomaly by manipulating the image on the screen, then use the computer for color correction, and make quality reproductions." This is just not so, and will not work.

This weakest link may have been strengthened. At an industry trade show the author saw a system that could rival and surpass any of the systems currently on the market.

This system is radically different from the conventional drum type systems. With the direct digital color separation system, most of the intricate settings of adjusting a drum type scanner are completely eliminated. The speed of this new and revolutionary system is short of unbelievable.

This basic separation system is not complicated, once the computer images are completed and "locked in."

The skill and accuracy of understanding color, from the moment that the computer is turned on, is totally in the eye, mind and the hands of the operator. "This is a totally new approach to color correction, a new technology," states Fred Morgan, of F and S, Inc., Columbus, GA, the inventor of this new system. "With our system we can prove what colors will be printed, no guess work, no subjectivity. Color is no longer elusive. The system is based on basic photographic masking principles."

DIRECT DIGITAL COLOR SEPARATIONS

The original idea, sketch, or drawing must be evaluated for tone values, depth of all colors, gray balance, shadow and highlight densities and screen rulings before the direct digital color separation program is started.

This is no different than if an artist were to use water color or oil. One basic advantage of this new system is that corrections in color can be made "at will" and "at once."

To simplify the operation, here are a few basic steps for computer art:

First, the artist draws his material, whether it is line work, solids or airbrush on the computer "drawing" board with a stylus. The computer, at prompt, will guide the artist every step of the way. If the artist wishes to use an airbrush effect he so advises the computer. With the push of a key he is in the airbrush mode. With another key he can change to drawing lines, whether straight, curved or circles, and again go back to airbrush.

The basic equipment for the artist is available from, but not limited to, IBM and Macintosh. TARGA© cards are available from the Truevision© Co. Double sided, double density 3.5" or 5.25" floppy disks suitable for color are required.

Digital color, or artwork is produced without a camera or optical lens. There is no need for a conventional camera or dark room since no light sensitive film is used in the initial computer art design stage. Yet the end result is the production of 4-color separated, screened films. All can be produced directly to color standards afforded the output device's color space. Once the artist has finished his work, the disk is sent to a direct digital color separation firm.

At the color separation house the process becomes even more simple. It remains under extreme accuracy and quality controls. The color corrected disk sends the stored color data to the

DIRECT DIGITAL COLOR SEPARATIONS

separation equipment and in minutes you have a set of four screened 4-color separations. A color correct proof is then made to guide the printer for proper color balance. In most cases, this entire color correction and separation operation can be completed in just a few minutes.

Matching the customer's product colors in print has always been challenging. There has been no way of accurately predicting how to match, in print, the actual color of some customer's products without much trial and error, making proof after proof to see if the color is right. When the job gets on press another set of problems may arise. The press color does not match the proof. WHAT DO YOU DO? F and S, Inc. developed a system that allows the matching of product colors on the first try. In beta testing their product, The Kolorist Color Matching System, (KCMS), has achieved 100% accuracy. The beta test site was a large textile manufacturer. The customer would "read" the specs for the actual product, which was a carpet, and KCMS told them the RGB values and CMYK dot percentages that were responsible for their carpet colors.

What is so unique to this system is that it is a color math model that is tied directly to the proofing system and the press. The system uses no color lookup tables and no color libraries. Some other systems use predetermined color libraries as reference colors to achieve what they call a "close match" of the colors needed.

No system is available, except KCMS, (patented) that uses a color math model to accurately predict color matches designed specifically to the printer's specific printing and proofing conditions. The KCMS system is available from F and S, Inc. Columbus, GA.

Basic Facts

Chapter 14

PUBLISHING & PRODUCTION EXECUTIVE

Screening Scene

Stochastic screening is a critical enabling technology for high-fidelity color

BY ROSE BLESSING AND ALEX HAMILTON

STOCHASTIC SCREENING facilitates the printing of jobs with more than four ink colors because it eliminates rosettes caused by screen angles. Sometimes it is spoken of as high-fidelity color technology because of its ability to render some tones more accurately than conventional screens, even within the gamut of four-color printing.

Stochastic screening products were launched in 1993 when Agfa introduced its CristalRaster and Linotype-Hell introduced its Diamond Screening.

TRADITIONAL SCREENS

With traditional screening, the imagesetter combines laser spots to "build" a halftone dot; the more spots, the larger the dot area. The maximum size of a single dot is a function of the screen ruling (or frequency), which forms a grid into which all the halftone dots fit and, therefore, determines the overall quality of the print. In traditional screening, the distance between the centers of the halftone dots remains constant.

For printing one-color jobs, the screen angle is set at 45 degrees to minimize its visual impact. Color printing is more complicated because the four screens must be aligned. There are two methods of overlaying the cyan, magenta, yellow and black screens: rational, including supercell and irrational tangent screening, which this article will not go into.

FM SCREENS

By contrast, frequency-modulated screening varies the number and placement of imagesetter spots in order to control ink coverage. Rather than combining spots to form a larger spot (for higher coverage), the laser images multiply spots in the vicinity of one another. Here the distance between the spot centers constantly varies.

Although some people call it "random" screening, stochastic is anything but that; the spots are placed very precisely to avoid forming patterns. It's also for this reason that the issue of screen angles becomes moot, because there are no longer any screening grids to align.

More recently, several suppliers have come out with "second order" stochastic systems, which combine elements of both traditional and FM screening. With this implementation, the marking engine combines laser spots and varies their placement in order to achieve the desired gray level.

Early criticisms of stochastic screening included surprisingly grainy highlights and plugged shadows, as well as difficulty creating proofs for a process with dots so tiny.

TECH TRENDS

Vendors of stochastic screening systems have responded by refining their processes. For example, Agfa added a third spot size, 30 microns to its 14- and 21- micron spots, and reports that the 14- micron spot is not necessary because its 21- micron-dot technology has been refined. Agfa has also addressed the problem of graininess in flat tints by adjusting the algorithm toward blue noise (from white) in the spectrum.

STOCHASTIC SCREENING

Linotype-Hell's Diamond Screening provides a similar range of spot sizes, from 15 to 40 microns. Spot sizes of 60, 80, and 100 microns are also possible for applications such as flexography and screen printing.

Some vendors, such as Barco Graphics, whose stochastic screening is called Monet, supply software that allows conventional screens and stochastic to be imaged on the same piece of film: Barco's software compensates the dot sizes to allow for expected dot gain with both types of screens.

Other screening solutions include:

- Adobe's Brilliant Screens
- DuPont's Lazel
- Harlequin's Dispersed Screening (HDS)
- Hyphen's FM
- Intellidot's Impression
- The Color Partnership's ICEfields
- PrePRESS Solutions' ESCOR FM
- Scitex's FULLtone
- Screen USA's Randot

Some non-stochastic screening solutions like TransCal's HiLine, are also marketed as suitable for high-fidelity color applications.

Printers venturing into stochastic screening technologies are "skating close to the edge of the carrying capacity of all the transfer media," repro film, plate and proofing materials, comments Mills Davis, Davis Inc., Washington, D.C. Therefore, to get the maximum benefits from the screening technologies, printers bringing such technologies into their work flows must be ready to pay careful attention to issues such as dot gain, use of appropriate films (high-contrast films to produce hard dots) and carefully chosen and carefully controlled proofing and platemaking methods.

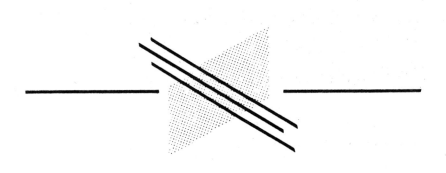

Basic Facts

Chapter 15

"LIVE" DEMONSTRATIONS

Oh, the misleading English language! There is a significant difference between a "live" model and a "live" equipment demonstration. Yet, at industry exhibits they both have their place, and yes, they are BOTH SPELLED "LIVE."

The type of exhibits and the products or equipment that are to be shown determine how the word "live" is used. In a survey of exhibitors, some interesting points were suggested.

At an exhibit, a cute model sits at the steering wheel of an earth-moving vehicle: DOES SHE SELL EARTH-MOVING VEHICLES? NO!

A model prances around a new version of an expensive automobile: DOES SHE SELL CARS? NO!

A model stands in an aisle blocking traffic, while pinning buttons on attendees: DOES SHE SELL ANYTHING? NO!

Do buyers or attendees remember the model when they return to their office to consider making a purchase? NO!

Does having a model at an exhibit, who hands out literature have any value? YES, INDEED! Someone should be doing this important activity. And it certainly should not be the president of the company. The president, however, might be available to talk to prospects, that is, if he is in his exhibit booth or on the exhibit floor.

Now, add to this scene, three girls (models) doing the hula or whatever, and you have lost the chance of having attendees asking questions about your product or service. Oh, the girl in the middle? Her phone number? Forget it!

A blaring audio or microphone will also chase attendees away from your exhibit area, as will annoying flashing strobe lights. All of these, if used properly, do have a place at an exhibit.

"LIVE" DEMONSTRATIONS

Nothing sells faster than for an attendee to actually see a product in action. Especially if the prospective buyer can touch some part of the product. Now, not all equipment is that easy to demonstrate. It is not possible to have a backhoe dig up an exhibit floor just to prove that it can perform as the literature claims.

In a "live" demonstration, the attendee should actually feel that he is part of the demonstration. This is especially true if an opportunity is presented to ask questions.

Giving out samples AFTER a demonstration is also a real incentive for the attendee to remember the company after returning home.

THE INDIVIDUAL EXHIBIT AREA

Money, money and more money is a basic factor in determining the size of an exhibit area. If yours is a live demonstration where attendees may sit down, make sure you provide ample space for this event. Attendees spilling into an aisle is a real no-no!

"LIVE" DEMONSTRATIONS

To this expense must be added the cost of many items such as personnel, exhibit furniture, signs, booth cleaning, booth setup, telephones, and services such as electricity and drainage, housing and travel, and a dozen more items, all sizable cost factors. Getting the exhibit in and out of the exhibit hall is a cost factor generally underestimated.

Here are a few suggestions that every exhibitor should take into consideration.

- Do not permit booth staff to "work" in the traffic aisles.
- Discourage models or sales people from going INTO AN AISLE while attempting to pin buttons on attendees while they are walking past a booth.
- If you spot a long-lost friend and you wish to talk to him, ask him into your booth location. The aisle is not a good place to have a conversation.
- Start your demonstrations on time. Attendees will walk out on a demonstration even if it is only a few minutes late.
- Make sure the staff knows where other staff members are. To be told that the person you want to see is "somewhere around" can turn off an attendee. If that person is out to lunch or busy talking to a prospect, say so.

LIVE DEMONSTRATIONS, PRODUCTS OR MODELS are very valuable and can be made to carry their cost. But it does pay to make a thorough study of the entire merchandising program back at the office, not when the show is about to start. The ultimate success of an industry exhibit comes down to one word. REHEARSE, REHEARSE, REHEARSE!

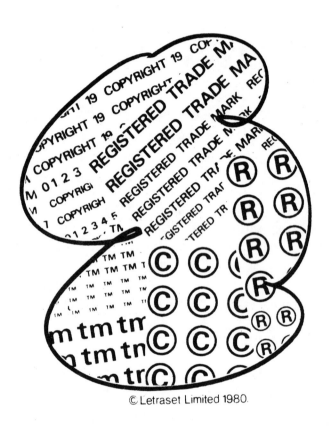
© Letraset Limited 1980.

TRADEMARKS: *Chapter* 16

THE OFFICIAL MEDIA GUIDE

TO THE MEDIA:

As the saying goes, "nobody's perfect." But, we can all strive for perfection. This guide is designed to help the media, in all forms, maintain high levels of accuracy in dealing with commonplace, everyday subject matter, trademarks.

Think of that for a moment and recognize that trademarks conceivable can be a part of virtually any article or feature one might write for magazines or trade journals or for any broadcast as well.

And the need for a reliable source goes beyond that, for authors of fiction and non-fiction books including dictionaries, and for editors, reporters, researchers, proofreaders, printers, advertising agencies, artists, designers, fact checkers and lexicographers.

This article, together with International Trademark Association's Trademark Checklist and Trademark Hotline, should be considered by the media as convenient sources to help determine not only whether a word is a trademark, but the correct way to spell it and the proper way to use it in language, both verbal and written.

TRADEMARKS: THE OFFICIAL MEDIA GUIDE

TRADEMARKS ARE PROPER ADJECTIVES AND SHOULD BE FOLLOWED BY GENERIC TERMS

Trademarks should be either CAPITALIZED completely, used with "Initial Caps" with quotes, or at the very least, with Initial Caps. Other alternatives for distinguishing trademarks include italic, boldface or different color type.

As a minimum requirement, use the generic term after the trademark at least once in each written communication and, when appropriate, in broadcast matter, preferably the first time the mark appears.

Examples:

>KLEENEX tissues
>"Life Savers" candy
>Kodak Cameras
>*VASELINE* petroleum jelly
>PAMPERS diapers
>Pizza Hut restaurants

Additional emphasis can be given to trademarks by using the word "brand" after the mark (SCOTCH Brand transparent tape) and/or by using one of the acceptable symbols that indicate trademark status. Some companies require the use of a trademark notice one or more times in all of their packaging, printed materials and advertising, namely:

> ® or Reg. U.S. Pat. & Tm. Off. if the mark is registered in the U.S. Patent and Trademark Office. TM (trademarks) or SM (service marks) for marks that are not registered.

> An asterisk (*) and a footnote that the mark is either "Reg. U.S. Pat. & Tm. Off." or if the mark is not registered, "A trade mark of X Company."

TRADEMARKS: THE OFFICIAL MEDIA GUIDE

TRADEMARKS SHOULD NOT BE PLURALIZED

Since trademarks are NOT nouns, they should not be used in plural form. Instead, pluralize the common nouns they describe.

Correct: Two SANKA decaffeinated coffees (or decafs).

Incorrect: Two SANKAS

Trademarks that end in "s" may be used with singular or plural nouns. Do not remove the "s" to singularize these marks.

TRADEMARKS SHOULD NOT BE USED IN THE POSSESSIVE FORM

Trademarks should never be used in the "'s" form, unless the trademark itself is possessive such as LEVI'S jeans, MCDONALD'S restaurants or JOHNSON'S baby shampoo.

TRADEMARKS ARE NEVER VERBS

Examples:

You can say "make six copies on the XEROX copier" or "Make a photocopy" but you CANNOT say "XEROX the report."

You can say "Polish my car with SIMONIZ paste wax" but you CANNOT say "SIMONIZ my car."

TRADEMARKS: THE OFFICIAL MEDIA GUIDE

TRADE NAMES AND TRADEMARKS ARE NOT THE SAME

Trademarks should not be confused with trade names, which are corporate or business names. Trade names are proper nouns. Trade names can be used in the possessive form and do not require a generic term. It is not appropriate to use a trademark symbol. Many companies use their trade names as trademarks.

Example:

> CORPORATE NAME: These athletic shoes are made by Reebok International Ltd.
>
> TRADE NAME: These athletic shoes are made by Reebok.
>
> TRADEMARK: Are you wearing REEBOK athletic shoes or another brand?

Trademarks are proper terms that identify the products and services of a business and distinguish them from the products or services of others. Trademarks can be a word, symbol, logo or design, or any combination of these.

If a mark is used improperly, it can end up as a generic name of the product or service, thereby losing its distinguishing function. It has happened man times in the past. Products such as linoleum, aspirin, escalator, cellophane, kerosene, mimeograph, and some surprising ones like trampoline, shredded wheat, and dry ice were originally trademarks which, improperly used and thereby unprotected, became the generic terms of those products.

TRADEMARKS: THE OFFICIAL MEDIA GUIDE

When a trademark becomes generic, anyone may use it. That will likely lead to several adverse situations. For one, consumers are literally robbed of the ability to repeat satisfactory purchases since there is no longer a clear identity of the product or service they want. And secondly, generic use literally destroys the owner's investment in its valuable asset.

To help prevent further and future genericide, to keep writers, editors, researchers, etc., on the right track and to avoid complaints about improper usage, the International Trademark Association has prepared the following guidelines.

The International Trademark Association, founded in 1978, is a not-for-profit membership organization committed to:

- promoting trademarks as essential to commerce throughout the world

- fulfilling a leadership role in public policy matters concerning trademarks

- educating business, the press and the public on the proper use and importance of trademarks

- provide an extensive range of informational and educational programs and services to its members.

For further information:

    The International Trademark Association
    1133 Avenue of the Americas
    New York, NY 10017
    Tel. 212-768-9887

THE IMPORTANCE OF A <u>TRADEMARK PROTECTION</u> CANNOT BE OVERLOOKED, AS IT OFTENTIMES IS THE MOST IMPORTANT FACTOR IN OBTAINING RELIEF FOR THE TRADEMARK OWNWER.

Robert E. Wagner
Wallenstein & Wagner
Chicago

Basic Facts — Chapter 17

Graphic Communications Business Practices

~

Established business practices form the basis of all plant-customer relations and are determining factors in any dispute or difference that may occur.(Stinson)

Graphic Communications Business Practices

1. Quotation. A quotation not accepted within 30 days may be changed.

2. Orders. Acceptance of orders is subject to credit approval and contingencies such as fire, water, strikes, theft, vandalism, acts of God, and other causes beyond the provider's control. Canceled orders require compensation for incurred costs and related obligations.

3. Experimental Work. Experimental or preliminary work performed at customer's request will be charged to the customer at the provider's current rates. This work cannot be used without the provider's written consent.

4. Creative Work. Sketches, copy, dummies and all other creative work developed or furnished by the provider are the provider's exclusive property. The provider must give written approval for all use of this work and for any derivation of ideas from it.

5. Accuracy of Specifications. Quotations are based on the accuracy of the specifications provided. The provider can re-quote a job at time of submission if copy, film, tapes, disks, or other input materials don't conform to the information on which the original quotation was based.

6. Preparatory Materials. Art work, type, plates, negatives, positives, tapes, disks, and all other items supplied by the provider remain the provider's exclusive property.

7. Electronic Manuscript or Image. It is the customer's responsibility to maintain a copy of the original file. The provider is not responsible for accidental damage to media supplied by the customer or for the accuracy of furnished input or final output. Until digital input can be evaluated by the provider, no claims or promises are made about the provider's ability to work with jobs submitted in digital format, and no liability is assumed for problems that may arise. Any additional translating, editing, or programming needed to utilize customer-supplied files will be charged at prevailing rates.

8. Alterations/Corrections. Customer alterations include all work performed in addition to the original specifications. All such work will be charged at the provider's current rates.

9. Prepress Proofs. The provider will submit prepress proofs along with original copy for the customer's review and approval. Corrections will be returned to the provider on a "master set" marked "O.K.," "O.K. With Corrections," or "Revised Proof Required" and signed by the customer. Until the master set is received, no additional work will be performed. The provider will not be responsible for undetected production errors if:
- proofs are not required by the customer;
- the work is printed per the customer's O.K.;
- requests for changes are communicated orally.

10. Press Proofs. Press proofs will not be furnished unless they have been required in writing in the provider's quotation. A press sheet can be submitted for the customer's approval as long as the customer is present at the press during makeready. Any press time lost or alterations/corrections made because of the customer's delay or change of mind will be charged at the provider's current rates.

74

Graphic Communications Business Practices

11. Color Proofing. Because of differences in equipment, paper, inks, and other conditions between color proofing and production pressroom operations, a reasonable variation in color between color proofs and the completed job is to be expected. When variation of this kind occurs, it will be considered acceptable performance.

12. Over-Runs or Under-Runs. Over-runs or under-runs will not exceed 10 percent of the quantity ordered. The provider will bill for actual quantity delivered within this tolerance. If the customer requires a guaranteed quantity, the percentage of tolerance must be stated at the time of quotation.

13. Customer's Property. The provider will only maintain fire and extended coverage on property belonging to the customer while the property is in the provider's possession. The provider's liability for this property will not exceed the amount recoverable from the insurance. Additional insurance coverage may be obtained if it is requested in writing, and if the premium is paid to the provider.

14. Delivery. Unless otherwise specified, the price quoted is for a single shipment, without storage, F.O.B. provider's platform. Proposals are based on continuous and uninterrupted delivery of the complete order. If the specifications state otherwise, the provider will charge accordingly at current rates. Charges for delivery of materials and supplies from the customer to the provider, or from the customer's supplier to the provider, are not included in quotations unless specified. Title for finished work passes to the customer upon delivery to the carrier at shipping point; or upon mailing of invoices for the finished work or its segments, whichever occurs first.

15. Production Schedules. Production schedules will be established and followed by both the customer and the provider. In the event that production schedules are not adhered to by the customer, delivery dates will be subject to renegotiation. There will be no liability or penalty for delays due to state of war, riot, civil disorder, fire, strikes, accidents, action of government or civil authority, acts of God, or other causes beyond the control of the provider. In such cases, schedules will be extended by an amount of time equal to delay incurred.

16. Customer-Furnished Materials. Materials furnished by customers or their suppliers are verified by delivery tickets. The provider bears no responsibility for discrepancies between delivery tickets and actual counts. Customer-supplied paper must be delivered according to specifications furnished by the provider. These specifications will include correct weight, thickness, pick resistance, and other technical requirements. Artwork, film, color separations, special dies, tapes, disks, or other materials furnished by the customer must be usable by the provider without alteration or repair. Items not meeting this requirement will be repaired by the customer, or by the provider at the provider's current rates.

17. Outside Purchases. Unless otherwise agreed in writing, all outside purchases as requested or authorized by the customer, are chargeable.

18. Terms/Claims/Liens. Payment is net cash 30 calendar days from date of invoice. Claims for defects, damages or shortages must be made by the customer in writing no later than 10

Graphic Communications Business Practices

calendar days after delivery. If no such claim is made, the provider and the customer will understand that the job has been accepted. By accepting the job, the customer acknowledges that the provider's performance has fully satisfied all terms, conditions, and specifications.

The provider's liability will be limited to the quoted selling price of defective goods, without additional liability for special or consequential damages. As security for payment of any sum due under the terms of an agreement, the provider has the right to hold and place a lien on all customer property in the provider's possession. This right applies even if credit has been extended, notes have been accepted, trade acceptances have been made, or payment has been guaranteed. If payment is not made, the customer is liable for all collection costs incurred.

19. Liability. *1. Disclaimer of Express Warranties:* Provider warrants that the work is as described in the purchase order. The customer understands that all sketches, copy, dummies, and preparatory work shown to the customer are intended only to illustrate the general type and quality of the work. They are not intended to represent the actual work performed.
2. Disclaimer of Implied Warranties: The provider warrants only that the work will conform to the description contained in the purchase order. The provider's maximum liability, whether by negligence, contract, or otherwise, will not exceed the return of the amount invoiced for the work in dispute. Under no circumstances will the provider be liable for specific, individual, or consequential damages.

20. Indemnification. The customer agrees to protect the provider from economic loss and any other harmful consequences that could arise in connection with the work. This means that the customer will hold the provider harmless and save, indemnify, and otherwise defend him/her against claims, demands, actions, and proceedings on any and all grounds. This will apply regardless of responsibility for negligence.
1. Copyrights. The customer also warrants that the subject matter to be printed is not copyrighted by a third party. The customer also recognizes that because subject matter does not have to bear a copyright notice in order to be protected by copyright law, absence of such notice does not necessarily assure a right to reproduce.

The customer further warrants that no copyright notice has been removed from any material used in preparing the subject matter for reproduction. To support these warranties, the customer agrees to indemnify and hold the provider harmless for all liability, damages, and attorney fees that may be incurred in any legal action connected with copyright infringement involving the work produced or provided.
2. Personal or economic rights. The customer also warrants that the work does not contain anything that is libelous or scandalous, or anything that threatens anyone's right to privacy or other personal or economic rights. The customer will, at the customer's sole expense, promptly and thoroughly defend the provider in all legal actions on these grounds as long as the provider:

• promptly notifies the customer of the legal action;
• gives the customer reasonable time to undertake and conduct a defense.

Graphic Communications Business Practices

The provider reserves the right to use his or her sole discretion in refusing to print anything he or she deems illegal, libelous, scandalous, improper or infringing upon copyright law.

21. Storage. The provider will retain intermediate materials until the related end product has been accepted by the customer. If requested by the customer, intermediate materials will be stored for an additional period at additional charge. The provider is not liable for any loss or damage to stored material beyond what is recoverable by the provider's fire and extended insurance coverage.

22. Taxes. All amounts due for taxes and assessments will be added to the customer's invoice and are the responsibility of the customer. No tax exemption will be granted unless the customer's "Exemption Certificate" (or other official proof of exemption) accompanies the purchase order. If, after the customer has paid the invoice, it is determined that more tax is due, then the customer must promptly remit the required taxes to the taxing authority, or immediately reimburse the provider for any additional taxes paid.

23. Telecommunications. Unless otherwise agreed, the customer will pay for all transmission charges. The provider is not responsible for any errors, omissions, or extra costs resulting from faults in the transmission.

What are "Business Practices"?

The term "Business Practices," as presented in this document reflects the common practices of the printing industry. However, "Business Practices" are not necessarily "recommended" practices. Some printers may elect to follow them; others may not. As each company drafts its own contractual provisions, it will also want to consider customers' wishes, relationships with potential customers, and other competitive issues. It is important to note that "Business Practices" having to do with rates, payment terms, and warranties may be subject to modification.

For more information, contact:

National Assn. of Printers & Lithographers
780 Palisade Ave., Teaneck, NJ 07666

Printing Industries of America, Inc.
100 Daingerfield Rd., Alexandria, VA 22314

Graphic Arts Technical Foundation
4615 Forbes Ave., Pittsburgh, PA 15213

Basic Facts   Chapter 18

federal register

Federal Trade Commission

16 CFR Part 310
Prohibition of Deceptive and Abusive Telemarketing Acts; Final Rule

New Telemarketing Sales Rule

New Telemarketing Sales Rule

While You Were Out

To: *Consumers*

Caller: *Federal Trade Commission*

Phone: *(202) 326-2222*

☐ **Telephoned** ☐ **Please Call**

☒ **Wants You To Know** ☐ **Returned Your Call**

Subject: *Consumer Protections -*
New Telemarketing Sales Rule

1. It is illegal for a telemarketer to call you if you have asked not to be called.
2. Calling times are restricted to the hours between 8 a.m. and 9 p.m.
3. Telemarketers must tell you it's a sales call, the name of the seller, and what they are selling before they make their pitch. If it's a prize promotion, they must tell you that no purchase or payment is necessary to enter or win.
4. It's illegal for telemarketers to misrepresent any information; any facts about their goods or services; earnings potential, profitability, risk, or liquidity of an investment; or the nature of a prize in a prize-promotion scheme.
5. Before you pay, telemarketers must tell you the total cost of the goods and any restrictions on getting or using them; or that a sale is final or non-refundable. In a prize promotion, they must tell you the odds of winning, that no purchase or payment is necessary to win, and any restrictions or conditions of receiving the prize.
6. It's illegal for a telemarketer to withdraw money from your checking account without your express, verifiable authorization.
7. Telemarketers cannot lie to get you to pay, no matter what method of payment you use.
8. You do not have to pay for credit repair, recovery room, or advance-fee loan/credit services until these services have been delivered.
9. It's illegal to help deceptive telemarketers if you know - or consciously avoid knowing - that they are breaking the law.
10. Your state law enforcement officers now have the power to prosecute fraudulent telemarketers who operate across state lines.

New Telemarketing Sales Rule

- Resist high pressure sales tactics. Legitimate businesses respect the fact that you're not interested.

- If you don't want the seller to call you back, say so. If they call back, hang up. They're breaking the law.

- Take your time. Ask for written information about the product, service, investment opportunity, or charity that's the subject of the call.

- Your financial investments may have consequences for people you care about. Before you respond to a phone solicitation, talk to a friend, family member, or financial advisor.

- Hang up if you're asked to pay for a prize. Free is free.

- Don't send money — cash, check or money order — by courier, overnight delivery, or wire to anyone who insists on immediate payment.

- Keep information about your bank accounts and credit cards to yourself — unless you know who you're dealing with.

- Before you pay, check out the company with your local consumer protection office.

- Hang up if a telemarketer calls before 8 a.m. or after 9 p.m.

- If you suspect a scam, call your state attorney general.

If you have a telephone, chances are you've been called by a telemarketer. Most phone sales pitches are made on behalf of legitimate organizations offering legitimate products or services. But many telephone sales calls are frauds. **The Federal Trade Commission** encourages consumers to be skeptical when they hear a phone solicitation.

The FTC's new Telemarketing Sales Rule will help protect consumers from abusive and deceptive telephone sales tactics. The rule empowers consumers to stop unwanted calls and gives state law enforcement officers the power to prosecute fraudulent telemarketers who operate across state lines.

For more information about consumer protections under the Telemarketing Sales Rule, write:

Bureau of Consumer Protection
Federal Trade Commission
Public Reference - Room 130
Washington, DC 20580

Telephone fraud is against the law.

Suspect a telephone scam? Call your state attorney general. If you've been victimized, call the National Fraud Information Center, 1-800-876-7060.

New Telemarketing Sales Rule

Stopping Telephone Scams

Phone: *(202) 326-2222*

Basic Facts   Chapter 19

GLOSSARY

FOR COMPUTER TERMS SEE END OF GLOSSARY

ACETATE
One of the transparent or translucent sheets used for artist's overlays. Similar to clear photographic film.

AIRBRUSH
A precision, compressed-air tool for spraying smooth areas of tones on artwork, and for retouching photographic prints or negatives.

ALBUMEN PLATE
One form of a lithographic plate. The printing image lies on the surface as compared to the recessed deep etch plate.

ALTERATIONS
Changes in the original manuscript copy made by the author after first proofs have been submitted to him by the typesetter, lithographer or computer operator.

ANTIQUE PAPER
Paper with a relatively rough or unfinished surface, not smooth, slick or coated.

ART
Original artwork, illustrations or photographs, reproduction proofs of type, hand-drawn lettering, or any other material ready for the lithographer's operation.

BACKBONE
The back edge of a book along which the sections of the book are bound.

GLOSSARY

BLEED
A printed page "bleeds" when edges of the actual printed area are purposely trimmed off in design or in cutting off to the finished size.

BLOCKING OUT
Eliminating any portion of a piece of art by painting out or masking out on the film or on the art.

BLUE PRINT
An inexpensive photo print made from the lithographer's negative to be used as a proof. Similar to a brown print except that the resultant proof is blue and white in color.

BROWN PRINT
Another photo print used as a rough proof. Made by exposing the lithographer's negative to special photographic paper. The resultant proof is brown and white in color.

CAMERA LUCIDA
An instrument used by the artist to trace a reproduction of an object to a piece of art on paper. A prism arrangement of mirrors projects the image onto the paper.

CIRCULAR SCALE
A circular tool for scaling art, type or photographs. The principle is the same as an engineering slide rule.

COLOR SEPARATION, DIRECT DIGITAL
A new state of the art system called the Kolorist Color Matching System, (F and S, Inc., Columbus, GA) can match, using 24 bit color boards, 16 million colors on most computers.

COLOR SKETCH
Rough drawing in color showing approximate size, position and colors of all units in a job to be lithographed.

CONTACT PRINT
A photographic print made with the negative or positive in contact with sensitized paper. No camera is necessary. Images are reversed, as from negative to positive, and prints can only be the same size as the original.

GLOSSARY

CONTINUOUS TONE
Art or its reproduction which has tonal graduation without the use of halftone dots.

COPY
Any material which is to be photographed or processed by the lithographer or computer operator, or otherwise prepared for a printing operation. The terms art and copy are generally used interchangeably.

CROPPING
Eliminating edges or portions of art and photographs that are not desired in the final reproduction.

DEEP ETCH
One form of a lithographic printing plate. Generally considered to be a more long life impression plate, meaning more impressions per plate. Positive transparencies are exposed on the press plate and the ink carrying areas are recessed slightly below the surface of the plate. This makes the printing area more "wear resistant."

DOT ETCHING
Changing or correcting the tone values on halftone negatives or positives by hand, usually with a brush or cotton swab, by altering the size of the halftone dots chemically.

DROPOUT
A halftone having no halftone screen dots in certain area highlights so that only the white paper shows when it is lithographed.

DUMMY
A preliminary drawing, layout or pasteup of a job showing a general position of the various items of the copy and art.

EMULSION
The light-sensitive coating on film, paper or even glass used in the lithographer's camera or other darkroom operations such as the making of contact prints.

FILM
A light-sensitive material used for recording a photographic image. See EMULSION.

GLOSSARY

FILTERS
　　Filters are used in camera operations for making color separations. Theoretically, a filter permits the photographing of one color at a time, regardless of the number of colors in the original art.

FLAT TONES
　　Lithographed areas of dot formations containing a single dot formation of a given screen value. All of the same screen size.

FOLIO
　　A page number given to sheets, such as a book. A type of index.

FUGITIVE
　　Ink colors that fade out to practically nothing. Window displays that lose a certain amount of color due to sunlight, heat or atmospheric conditions.

GANG RUNS
　　A common practice in printing plants where a multiple of different jobs are printed on the same sheet, eliminating the making of separate printing plates.

GRAINING
　　The roughening of a metal lithographic printing plate prior to exposure of any subject matter such as art or copy film.

GRAY SCALE
　　This is a scale which has tone values (gradation) ranging from white to black. It is used as a guide to measure tonal values by cameramen, photographers and retouchers.

GRIPPER MARGIN
　　The amount of paper along the front edge of a press sheet that is needed for the press grippers to pull the sheet through the press. A common figure is one-quarter of an inch although certain presses may have different specifications.

HALFTONE
　　A reproduction of a photograph or other subject that has highlights, shadows and intermediate tone values. The various tone values are obtained by breaking up the image into a graduated series of dot patterns. This process may be performed by placing a cross-ruled screen between the camera lens and the film before exposure. For a different method see STOCHASTIC SCREENING.

GLOSSARY

HIGHLIGHTS
The lightest or whitest portion of any art that shows a range of tones ranging from white to black.

IMPOSITION
The position of pages or other copy on a press plate so that when the job is lithographed cut and folded, the pages are in proper reading or binding order.

KEY
To identify and locate positions of art in a dummy or mounting by means of alphabetical or numerical symbols.

LINE COPY
Any original art to be photographed that is made up of solids, lines or dots and are not made up of tonal gradations such as "wash drawings."

MAKEREADY
All of the preparation of adjusting the printing press and preparing the plate position, ink requirements, etc., prior to starting to print the job.

MATTE
A non-shiny, dull rough surface. Such as that of an artist's drawing board.

MECHANICAL BINDING
Binding which holds a book or a group of pages together by metal or plastic rings, staples or spirals. "Perfect Binding" is not considered as mechanical. See SIDE WIRE, also PERFECT BINDING.

MIDDLE TONES
The range of tones between highlights and shadows of a photograph.

MOIRE
A most objectionable pattern caused by making a halftone of a halftone reproduction or by incorrect screen angles in color printing.

MULTI-COLOR
Generally described as lithographing a job in more than two colors.

GLOSSARY

NEGATIVE
A photographic image of original copy on paper or film in which the relationship of left and right, light and shade are reversed from those of the original subject. Positive reading prints are made from negatives.

OFFSET BLANKET
The rubber covering of the press cylinder that receives the lithographic image from the plate cylinder and transfers the image to the paper during the printing operation.

OUTLINING
Eliminating background areas of photographs. This system may be accomplished by hand or by airbrush.

OVERLAY
Generally, a transparent sheet placed over art copy or photographs which permits grease pencil marking for indicating color or other information that will be used as the job progresses through the printing plant.

PAGINATION
The numbering of pages for a book or magazine.

PERFECT BINDING
A method of binding together a series of loose pages. Technically, a group of pages, usually more than 50, where the cover and the inside pages are "glued" together without using a cloth backbone strip, staple or thread. There are several patented methods available.

PHOTOCOMPOSING
The technique of placing many images on a printing plate for running a job in multiples, such as can labels. There is no set rule as to the variety of multiple images that may be on the same plate.

PHOTOLETTERING
Composing letters into words on a machine that photographs letters and assembles the images of them as one negative. A "Photosetter."

PHOTOMONTAGE
A unit of art that consists of a combination of various photographs or parts of photographs, that when completed, will make one final composite picture.

GLOSSARY

PHOTOSTAT
A photographic copy of any subject made directly on paper or film by the patented "Photostat" machine. Copy may be enlarged, reduced or screened. There are a number of similar machines that have their own patents and methods of operation.

PLATE/CYLINDER
A sheet or cylinder of metal or plastic, that carries the images such as type, drawings, photographs which are to be reproduced by any of several printing methods.

POSITIVE
A photographic image on paper, or film which corresponds to the original subject in all details of appearance. The opposite of a negative.

PRESS PROOFS
Press proofs are generally considered to be "pulled" on a production press. However, there are proofing presses that pull proofs "by hand" although they are under full electric power. PROGRESSIVE PROOFS are those where individual colors are made and examined one color at a time. Once approved, all colors may be "pulled" one over the other making a complete composite proof.

PRINT AND TUMBLE
Printing a press sheet with the front and back of a job on the same press plate. When one side of the press sheet is printed, it is turned over from gripper to back so the final printed press sheet, when cut in half, yields two completely printed pieces.

PROCESS INK
Ink made specially for process color reproduction. Usually the three primary colors, yellow, red and blue and the key color, black. NOT ALL ink colors on a printer's shelf are suitable for process printing.

PROGRESSIVE PROOFS
See PRESS PROOFS.

REGISTER
The fitting together of all of the components of a job, such as colors or position of artwork on a page. Also to register the printing of work on the backup of a printed sheet.

GLOSSARY

REPRODUCTION PROOFS
Corrected proofs of type copy or art suitable as clean, sharp copy for the lithographer's camera.

REVERSE
An image in which the black and white areas are exchanged from those of the original subject, but the relationship of left to right is the same as the original subject. Actually, it is a white image on a black or colored background. Reverses can also be enlarged, reduced or screened during this operation. Certain small letters, such as six point and certain heavily serifed letters, are not suited for reverse use. These cause poor readability.

SADDLE BINDING
A form of mechanical binding by stitching wire (staples) through the middle of a group of sheets after they have been collated and folded.

SCALING
Determining the correct size of reduction or enlargement of type or art work before actual reproduction or other operations in the lithographer's plant.

SCREEN
A cross-ruled sheet of glass or film which is placed between the film which is to receive an image and the camera lens to obtain dot formations in halftones. See STOCHASTIC SCREENING.

SEWED BINDING
Binding by sewing signatures of sheets as they are gathered to form a book of multiple signatures.

SHADOWS
The darkest or most shaded portions of a subject which shows a range of tones from white to black. Usually in a photograph. See WASH DRAWING.

SIDE WIRE BINDING
A mechanical form of binding. This is done by stapling from front to back at the left-hand edge, after the pages of a magazine or book are gathered in their correct sequence. Some books or magazines have two staples while others may have three.

GLOSSARY

SILVER PRINT
See BROWN PRINT.

STRIPPING
Assembling photographic negatives or positives and fastening them, in correct position, to either a sheet of paper or acetate base which is used in making a press plate.

STOCHASTIC SCREENING
A screening technique, unlike the standard halftone screening method. Stochastic uses small 14 to 30 micron dots or commonly called spots, to compose an image. These random sized dots appear in an irregular manner yet, on the printing plate and printed sheet, they are always in the same position (register for color printing.)

SWATCH
A sample of color, ink, cloth or paper, which is to be matched for the printing operation.

TRANSPARENCIES
A transparent positive photograph in black and white or color.

TWO-UP
A common term to designate the number of subjects on the same plate. "Four-up," "Six-up," etc.

VANDYKE
See BROWN PRINT.

VARNISHING, OR COATING
A coating of a lithographed job with a transparent varnish to give it a glossy finish. While it gives a more glossy finish, it also offers a dust and wear resistant coating. Instead of a "liquid" coating, sometimes a plastic coating is used. This is called laminating. Varnishing (coating) may be done either on-press or off-press depending on the lithographer's equipment.

WASH DRAWING
An art form of creating various tone values from white to black by using an artist brush as opposed to a mechanical system. An airbrush may be used also.

GLOSSARY

WORK AND TURN
 See PRINT AND TUMBLE. With work and turn, the printed sheets are turned over from the first printing for the backup printing operation but using the SAME FRONT gripper edge.

WATERLESS PRINTING
 A new method of printing by the lithographic process that eliminates the need for dampening the printing plate. The normal dampening (water rollers) are removed or disengaged. The press itself must be reconfigured by the press manufacturer with very precise temperature controlled rollers. Special inks are also required with this process.

~ ~ ~

As with most glossaries, there are a multitude of definitions that are left out. Perhaps this is why WEBSTER has so many revised editions. This book lists only those definitions that have been in general practice over many years, with the exception of Stochastic and Waterless which are ultra modern day systems.

The author recommends the following publications for more detailed COMPUTER TERMS.

• Revised COMPLETE DICTIONARY OF GRAPHIC ARTS TERMINOLOGY by Harvey R. Levenson, Ph.D., Department Head, Graphic Communications Dept., California Polytechnic State University, San Luis Obispo, CA 93407.

• DICTIONARY OF COMPUTER TERMS by Douglas Downing and Michael Covington. BARRON'S Educational Series, 250 Wireless Blvd., Hauppauge, NY 11788. Fourth Edition, 1000 key terms. Also available at bookstores.

Basic Facts — Chapter 20

PARTIAL LIST PREPRESS TERMS

additive primaries
Red, green, and blue light that, together, produce white light. Compare with subtractive primaries.

alpha channel
An 8-bit channel reserved by some image-processing applications for masking or additional color information.

anti-aliasing
The rendering of hard-edged objects so they blend smoothly into the background. A technique for merging object-oriented art into bitmaps.

artifact
A visible indication (defect) in an image, caused by limitations in the reproduction process (hardware or software).

ASCII
(American Standard Code for Information Interchange) A standard format for representing digital information in 8-bit chunks.

banding
A visible stair-stepping of shades in a gradient.

Bezier curves
In object-oriented programs, a curve whose shape is defined by anchor points set along its arc.

bit
(Binary Digit) The smallest unit of information in a computer. It can define by itself one of two conditions (on or off).

bitmapped
An image formed by a rectangular grid of pixels. The computer assigns a value to each pixel, from one bit of information (black or white), to as much as 24 bits per pixel for full color images.

byte
A unit of measure equal to eight bits of digital information (2^3). The standard unit measure of file size. See also megabyte, kilobyte, and gigabyte.

camera-ready art
Any artwork or type that is ready to be prepared for printing.

calibration
Setting equipment to a standard measure to produce reliable results.

GLOSSARY • PREPRESS TERMS

calibration bars
On a negative, proof or printed piece, a strip of tones used to check printing quality.

CIE
(Commission Internationale de l'Eclairage) An international group that has developed a set of color definition standards endorsed by Adobe for PostScript Level 2.

CMYK
(cyan, magenta, yellow, black) The subtractive primaries, or process colors, used in color printing. Black (K) is usually added to enhance color and to print a true black.

color correction
The process of adjusting an image to compensate for scanner deficiencies or for the characteristics of the output device.

color picker
A utility for specifying colors on the monitor.

color proof
A representation of what the final printed composition will look like. The resolution and quality of different types of color proofs can vary greatly.

color separation
The division of an image into its component colors for printing. Each color separation is a piece of negative or positive film.

color transparency
A photographic image on transparent film used as artwork. 35mm, 4"x5" and 8"x10" formats are commonly used.

comp
Comprehensive artwork used to present the general color and layout of a page. See proof.

contrast
The relationship between the lightest and darkest areas of an image.

crop marks
Lines printed showing the dimensions of the final printed page. These marks are used for final trimming.

CT
(Continuous Tone) A file format used for exchanging high-level scan information.

DCS
(Desktop Color Separation) A format which creates five PostScript files for each color image.

densitometer
A device sensitive to the density of light transmitted or reflected by paper or film. It is used to check the accuracy, quality, and consistency of output.

density
The degree of opacity of a photographic image on paper or film.

dithering
The process of specifying color to adjacent pixels in order simulate a third color in a bitmapped image. This technique is used when a full range of colors is not available.

Dmax
The highest level of density on a film negative.

dot gain
A printing defect in which dots print larger than intended, causing darker colors or tones.

dpi
(Dots Per Inch) A measure of the output resolution produced by printers, imagesetters or monitors.

GLOSSARY • PREPRESS TERMS

elliptical dot
A type of halftone screen dot with an elliptical rather than circular shape, which sometimes produces better tonal gradations.

emulsion
The coating of light-sensitive material on a piece of film.

emulsion down
This specifies a readable film image with the emulsion side facing away from the viewer. The printer usually decides whether emulsion should be up or down.

EPS
(Encapsulated PostScript) A file format used to transfer PostScript image information from one program to another.

film
A transparent material coated with a light-sensitive substance.

film negative
A piece of film with a reversed image, in which dark areas appear white, and vice versa.

four-color process
The use of cyan, magenta, yellow, and black in printing to produce a wide variety of colors.

gamma
The measure of how compressed or expanded dark or light shades become in an image.

gamma correction
Compressing or expanding the ranges of dark or light shades in an image.

GCR
(Gray Component Replacement) A technique for reducing the amount of cyan, magenta and yellow in an area and replacing them with an appropriate level of black.

gradation
A smooth transition between black and white, one color and another, or color and the lack of it.

grayscale
The depiction of gray tones between black and white. A grayscale monitor is able to display distinct gray pixels as well as black and white ones, but not color pixels.

halftone screen
A pattern of dots of different sizes used to simulate a continuous tone photograph, either in color or black and white.

hard dot
A dot in a halftone screen that has smooth, crisp edges.

highlight
The lightest part of an image.

HLS
A color model based on three co-ordinates: hue, lightness (or luminance) and saturation.

HSV
A color model based on three co-ordinates: hue, saturation and value.

hue
The wavelength of light of a color in its purest state (without the addition of white or black).

GLOSSARY • PREPRESS TERMS

imagesetter
A device used to output a computer image or composition at high resolution onto photographic paper or film.

kilobyte
(K, KB) A unit of measure of digital information corresponding to 1024 bytes. Abbreviated and referred to as K.

knockout
A shape or object printed by eliminating (knocking out) all background colors. Contrast to overprinting.

LAN
(Local Area Network) A group of connected computers in a relatively small area that share access to printers and other peripheral devices.

lpi
(Lines Per Inch) A measure of the frequency of a halftone screen (usually ranging from 55-200). Originally, halftones were made by placing an etched glass plate over an image and exposing it to produce dots. Lpi refers to the frequency of the horizontal and vertical lines.

luminosity
A value corresponding to the brightness of color.

LUT
(Look-Up Table) The table of colors a computer can display at a given time. The computer uses the table to approximate the desired color from the range it has available.

MacPaint
A common format on the Macintosh computer for storing and transferring low-resolution, monochromatic bit-mapped images. It originated with the paint application of the same name.

mask
The inactive area of a bitmapped image which will not respond to changes.

megabyte
(MB) A unit of measure of stored data corresponding to 1,024 kilobytes, or 1,048,576 bytes.

moiré
An undesirable artifact produced in printing when halftone screen patterns become visible. This is often caused by misaligned screens.

monitor calibration
The process of correcting the color rendition settings of a monitor to match selected colors of printed output.

monochrome
A black-and-white display with no gray tones.

negative See film negative.

object-oriented
A type of drawing that defines an image mathematically rather than as pixels in a bitmap.

overprinting
Printing over areas already printed. Contrast to knockout.

PICT/PICT2
A common format for defining bitmapped or object-oriented images on the Macintosh. The more recent format (PICT2) supports 24-bit color.

pigment
Particles that absorb and reflect light and appear colored to our eyes. The substance that gives ink its color.

GLOSSARY • PREPRESS TERMS

pixel
(Picture Element) The smallest distinct unit of a bitmapped image displayed on a screen.

PMS
(Pantone Matching System) A commonly used system for identifying specific ink colors.

posterization
The deliberate constraint of a gradation into visible steps as a special effect.

ppi
(Pixels Per Inch) A measure of the amount of scanned information. The finer the optics of the scanner, the higher the scan resolution.

process colors
The four colors (cyan, magenta, yellow and black) that are combined to print a wide range of colors. When blended, these reproduce only a small portion of all the colors found in nature, but they can reproduce the widest range with the fewest inks when printing. See also CMYK.

proof
A reasonably accurate sample of how a finished piece is intended to look. Proofs can be in black and white or color.

RAM
(Random Access Memory) The memory a computer needs to store the information it is processing at any given moment. This is short-term memory and is lost when the power is shut off.

rasterization
The process of converting mathematical and digital information into a series of dots by an imagesetter for the production of negative or positive film.

registration marks
Small cross-hairs on film used in the alignment of negatives.

registration
The alignment of different films or printing plates to produce one printed image.

reflective art
Artwork prepared so that it may be photographed or input into a computer by scanning.

reflective densitometer
Instrument used to measure the density on paper.

RGB
(Red, Green, Blue) The additive primary colors used for computer monitor displays. See also additive primaries.

RIP
(Raster Image Processor) Part of an output device that rasterizes information so that it may be imaged onto film or paper.

rosette
The pattern created when all four color halftone screens are placed at the traditional angles.

saturation
The amount of gray in a color. The higher the gray content, the lower the saturation.

scanner
A device used to digitize images to be manipulated, output, or stored on a computer.

screen angles
The angles used to offset the different films in process color separations. Proper screen angles are critical to minimize moiré patterns.

GLOSSARY • PREPRESS TERMS

screen frequency
The number of lines or dots per inch on a halftone screen.

service bureau
A business that specializes in outputting computer files on laser image-setters.

soft dot
A type of dot in a halftone screen whose edge is not smoothly circular. This can create a fuzzier image. By contrast, a hard dot has a very smooth edge.

stripping
The preparation and assembling of film prior to platemaking.

subtractive primaries
The inks (cyan, magenta, and yellow) used in printing to create different colors. In contrast to additive primaries, these produce darker colors when combined.

Targa
(TGA) A file format for exchanging 24-bit color files on PCs.

TIFF
(Tagged Image File Format) A file format for exchanging bitmapped images (usually scans) between applications.

transmissive densitometer
Instrument used to measure the coverage of exposed film.

trapping
A prepress technique which allows for variation in registration during the press run. On the desktop, this is done primarily by allowing an overlap between abutting colors.

UCR
(Undercolor Removal) A technique for reducing the amount of magenta, yellow and cyan in neutral areas and replacing them with an appropriate amount of black.

~

GLOSSARY • PREPRESS TERMS

Glossary reprinted with permission of Agfa, Division of Bayer Inc. from "Introduction to Digital Color Prepress."

DISCLAIMER

The names, initials, or reference to Lord & Taylor, USA TODAY, Harris, The New York Times, The Wall Street Journal, Mazda, Hertz, Digital, Diners Club, Akiyama, Southern Bell, Franklin Printing Co., Mueller-Martini, Chrysler, ADWEEK, Ogilvy and Mather, Arizona, Agfa-Bayer, William Strunk, Jr., IBM, N.J.S.A.C.O.P., Macintosh, Truevision, CristalRaster, GATF, Linotype-Hell, Barco Graphics (Monet), PIA, NAPL, NPES, ASAE, etc., all may be copyrighted entities in their own right. The use of such entity in this book is for illustration purposes only. No infringement is suggested nor intended. W.J.S.